Women, Law,
and the Genesis Traditions

to David
Daube

•

CALUM M.
CARMICHAEL

WOMEN, LAW,
AND THE
GENESIS
TRADITIONS

EDINBURGH
UNIVERSITY
PRESS

.

CONTENTS

•

cop. 3

The publisher is grateful to
the Hull Memorial Publication Fund
of Cornell University
for a grant towards
costs of this
volume.

·

INTRODUCTION

I suppose it is a rather startling thesis to claim that certain laws in the Deuteronomic legislation are about many of the women we meet in the book of Genesis. One does not expect legislation to have this kind of relationship to literary traditions. Laws, apparently, are just not constructed this way. Any conventional textbook on Jurisprudence will list the sources of law in a legal system. For example, a textbook on biblical jurisprudence might list, among other sources, an assembly, native or foreign, an oracle, a custom, but it is not likely to cite the exploration of traditional lore concerning the exploits of a nation's ancestry as providing a source. Yet a process by which legal questions have been put to problems in ancient Hebrew tradition is what explains the origin of many laws in Deuteronomy.

To prepare the reader for the presentation of this view certain features about the Deuteronomic laws and the Genesis stories are worth noting at the outset. In regard to the former, no legislation invites so much questioning as that contained in Deuteronomy. A persistently puzzling quality characterises its various rules. To be sure, because these rules are found in the bible, long familiarity with them, and perhaps a misplaced reverence, have detracted from an appreciation of their intriguing quality. Commentators, ancient and modern, seem to see nothing very surprising about laws prohibiting an ox and an ass ploughing together, against muzzling an ox when it is treading grain, and against killing a mother bird along with its eggs or young. A little probing, however, raises serious doubts about taking these laws at face value. Many other rules in the code also raise questions about how this lawgiver has arrived at his constructions. Why does he bother to prohibit the renovation of a marriage ? What prompts him to legislate for the extraordinary case of a man who falsely accuses his wife of not being a virgin on her wedding night ? Why is he concerned with a rather rare problem of inheritance affecting a first-born son by a wife whom the husband detests, who does not appear to have been divorced by him, and where his affections lie with another son by a second wife whom he favours? The narrow scope of many of the laws is one of their most puzzling features. Fortunately, this narrowness provides one of the major clues for making inroads on the problem. It also leads us, for the laws just cited, for example, to the women of the Genesis stories.

To refer to the latter as stories is neither revealing nor sophisticated. What we find is rather a complex mix of legends, sagas, even lawgiving, and, above all, tales (aetiological myths) invented long after the events in question but recorded as the events themselves with a view to explaining and even justifying them. Within this mix unified themes are to be found. Indeed a strong sense of historical continuity, with an intense interest in beginnings, either in national or in pre-national history, gives to the entire material a shape and importance that the modern reader might too easily overlook. A close scrutiny of it is justified, not because of what the bible has become, but because this literature meant so much to those whose heritage it constituted. There is a sophistication about every part of the book, an attention to detail, a consciousness of meaning, which should never be under-estimated. A consequence, which is important for research purposes, is that not just the sum of the parts but the parts themselves would have received ever recurring attention from the ancient Israelites. For example, there is every reason to expect that the role of women in the various stories, what they do, or what happens to them, would have invited much reflection. That is to say, the Genesis material itself has incorporated some of the results of this process of critical reflection, but equally important, this process would have continued long after the book attained its final shape. What we are faced with is the complex phenomenon of national consciousness, sometimes dormant, sometimes intense, but always existing in some shape or form over long stretches of time, and focused on certain events and persons of the past.

To plot over time the high and low points of this communal sense of identity is a well-nigh impossible task. There is probably a link between an awareness of this identity and committing age-old traditions to writing, with the latter activity reflecting a heightened sense of the former. Solomonic times (*circa* 950 B.C.) seem to be important for much of the *literary* activity that has gone into the composition of Genesis. With the passage of another one hundred years the book may have attained its final shape. The work that has become the book of Deuteronomy is later again and probably belongs to the seventh century B.C.

In a previous book I proposed a solution to the long-standing problem of the seemingly haphazard, even chaotic, arrangement of the Deuteronomic laws.[1] A central concern was to demonstrate the many links that existed between these laws and literary traditions in other books of the bible, especially but not at all exclusively in the book of Genesis. To appreciate how the lawgiver moved from one topic to the next in his law code, it was often necessary to observe how the topic itself was suggested by some aspect of a tradition which in turn contained another and quite different one which aroused his interest. Many examples of this procedure were noted (although many others escaped me at the time). One question that I barely touched on was to ask why a lawgiver should resort to such a process of constructing laws. A major aim of the present work is an attempt to answer this question. Should it succeed, we shall have uncovered a probably unique method by which new rules of law came into existence.

The demonstration of the proposed thesis proceeds on the basis of a limited number of Genesis traditions: those involving incidents in which women play an important role. It will be observed that time and again the lawgiver has taken stock of such occurrences, has noted how frequently they involve similar matters, has not liked what he has seen, and has addressed himself to the issues raised. One major motivation underlying his work is to uphold the honour and dignity of women, an aim accompanied by an acute sense of Israel's nationhood. He is not reforming the fundamental structure of society in which he lives and which from a modern perspective is doubtless characterised by the restrictive, even repressive, position of women. Rather he is conscious of their humiliating treatment in those Genesis stories and he is moved first to identify the wrongs in question, and then to counteract them according as they might appear in a more conventional form in his time.

What he does is not without precedent in the Genesis traditions themselves. In their final shape the process has already begun. The outraged attitude of the two brothers of Dinah to her treatment at the hands of Shechem is a major feature of that narrative. The negative attitude to Lot's proposed treatment of his two daughters can be discerned in the sequel to the story of the destruction of Sodom and Gomorrah. The phenomenon in question, increasing reflection involving greater sensitivity to features in previous tradition, is found both in other parts of the bible and in other cultures. The book of Ruth, in harking back and borrowing from certain Genesis traditions, reveals in the subtle connections forged by its author much reflection on the position of the women in those traditions. In Greek material, whereas certain myths involving women, Iphigeneia and Clytemnestra, for example, reveal little or no awareness of their personal standing, the matter is quite different in the tragedies.

Once the basic premise is accepted the thesis put forward in the following pages is relatively easy to prove. The premise is that the source of the problems taken up in the Deuteronomic legislation is not, as is almost universally thought, matters that arose in the everyday life of the Israelites at various times and places, but matters that are found in the literary traditions available to the legislator in his time. Instead of having to infer what the problems were in real life, we can point to them in written sources known to us. It is this link between law and literature rather than between law and life which explains why many of the laws are hypothetical in character. The importance of this result is perhaps to be viewed in light of the new understanding of the hypothetical, paradigmatic character of ancient Near Eastern law codes.[2]

The lawgiver's method is one in which legal and ethical questions are addressed to the problems he comes upon in the ancient traditions. Judicial constructions then follow. His procedure is at one level simple and at another complicated. Problems with which the traditions themselves are concerned are duly taken up by the lawgiver. In doing so, however, he is faced with the task of rethinking them so that they are both more intelligible and more relevant to his own time and place. This means that he has to shed them of their non-Israelite features and transform the idiosyncratic bias that is central to a tradition into something more manageable for his legal purposes. One primary motivation for so proceeding must have been the confusion that arose in the minds of later hearers of the traditions as to the conduct or treatment of figures who had taken on legendary qualities, Abraham, Sarah, Jacob, Leah, Judah, for example. The lawgiver's stance is essentially a critical one. He is, as he sees it, and as we would judge too, bringing loftier standards of law and morality to bear upon certain matters in the traditions, critical judgments upon both the patriarchs and matriarchs of the nation. No longer can we say, as C.H. Gordon does,[3] that in the bible Sarah and Dinah, for example, are never condemned for some of their actions. The inevitable tension created by the clash between his critical approach and the high regard in which these national heroes and heroines would be held explains some of the most puzzling and surprising laws in his code.

The complexity of the lawgiver's task, purging confusion in the understanding of what exactly is going on in these early traditions, laying out the comparable problems in a contemporary setting, is illumined by a statement in Deut 1:17: 'Thou shalt not be partial in judgment; thou shalt hear the small and the great alike; thou shalt not be afraid of the face of man, for the judgment is God's, and the case that is too hard for thee, thou shalt bring to me, and I will hear it.' There is a very real sense in which the many cases taken up from the Genesis traditions constitute difficult ones that have been solved by Moses before, according to the book of Deuteronomy, he presents his laws to the Israelites. He has, moreover, in judging the great ones of his nation shown no partiality.

Why, we might ask, has the Deuteronomist gone in for the fiction of attributing his laws to Moses? The answer is that this legendary figure of some five hundred years (at a very rough estimate) before his time was indeed associated with lawgiving, but his many laws were not known and had to be deduced. The Deuteronomist is acquainted with the laws in the book of the Covenant (Ex 21:1-23:19), as well as with the ten commandments (Ex 20:1-17), and these will have been regarded long before his time as Mosaic. But Moses' life work had been to take the Israelites to a new land and surely, so the belief would run (and existing tradition would have supported it), he had been concerned with the requirements and ideals necessary for living in that land. His own ancestors, Abraham, Isaac, and Jacob, had experienced life there. (Some of the Genesis narratives record their adventures as an anticipation of the later national settlement in Canaan.) Moses, being a lawgiver, would have looked back on their experiences (some of them involving disputes and their resolution), and with a critical eye made judgments based upon them. What he learned would have been put in the form of laws. These the Deuteronomic author had been able to work out because, confident that he could assume the mind of Moses in many matters, he was in a position to review the same traditions that Moses knew. Whether or not these actually were the same is irrelevant.

The results obtained by noting how the problems that are an integral part of the literature inspire the construction of later laws lead, as has already been noted, to an interesting observation about the nature of the literature itself. In its final shape it too shows a definite tendency to be concerned at the reflective moral and legal level with the very problems that doubtless inspired the origin of the literature in the first place. The stories underwent revisions because the revisers began to address the problems in the stories. Either they reshape the material so that the problems are brought out more clearly, as in Shechem's seduction of Dinah (it is no accident that her name, like Shechem's and Hamor's, is artificial – it means Judgment), or they are played down, as in Abraham and Isaac's treatment of their wives. Or, again, by arranging the presentation of their material so that one story is made to relate to another, as in the placement of the story about Lot's seduction by his daughters shortly after a story involving his offer of them to a male mob, the revisers of these ancient traditions show a keen moral and legal awareness. It is beyond the scope of this study to probe this obviously important area,[4] but it is clear that the Deuteronomist's own procedure is simply a continuation of one that already had a considerable history.

The study also brings out some interesting links between law and religion. It can be shown that in a large number of instances in which a problem in life is handled by the deity at an earlier stage of development, at a later stage this same problem, which has been recorded in a tradition, receives the attention of the Deuteronomic legislator. His aim is two-fold. He recognises that because of the deity's intervention the recipients of such traditions are confused about what the recorded problem is, and how it should be handled in their situation in life. He first seeks to clarify the issue in question, or to present one that approximates the one raised in the tradition. Secondly, he imposes a solution which may or may not chime with the deity's transmitted one. The earlier stage represents a theological attempt to address problems and an advance is achieved at the later stage because the matter can be handled legally. The theological activity is no less important because of such an advance. It indicates that a problem has been identified but obstacles of one kind or another (usually the absence of workable legal machinery) have prevented a concrete solution.

Another result of the study, as has been mentioned, is the connection that is found to exist between a strong sense of national identity and a concern with the status of women. Why should there be such a link? Ordinarily our sense of attachment to our native country is little reflected upon, especially if we are living within the country and contact with foreign nations is minimal. Moreover, we do not need to justify belonging to our nation in a way that is required of us if we belong to, say, a political party or a religious group. Once, however, for whatever reason, there is conscious reflection upon what it means to be a national of a certain country criteria of belonging are established. The reason why in Deuteronomy awareness of nationhood goes hand in hand with sensitivity to raising the status of women is readily explained. Almost all of the laws involving them issue from reflection upon and response to the situations of women whose humiliating treatment was invariably at the hands of members of foreign groups. Moreover, the humiliation they experienced was traceable not just to a foreign group but to the ancestors of the Israelite nation themselves. Not only were these ancestors sometimes the initial cause of their humiliation but foreign women were treated badly, or were seen as being treated badly by them (for example, Laban so viewed Jacob's action with his daughters, Rachel and Leah).

The Deuteronomist's own time was doubtless one of considerable international activity. His wisdom background, which is also characterised by an international outlook, is much involved in questions of sexual morality, an inevitable development in a setting in which young men are the focus of attention. His immersion in the wisdom tradition and his sense of belonging to his own nation in the midst of others would incline him to focus on the incidents involving women in the Genesis traditions, and these events in turn would enhance his concern with national identity and higher standards of sexual morality. Both the Deuteronomist's nationalism and his wisdom background have been increasingly uncovered in recent research.[5] Their influence on his review of the women who belong to the formative stage of his nation's history has not.

SARAH

No less than three narratives in Genesis recount the strange case of
a patriarch's passing his wife off as his sister.[1] In each incident the
patriarch feels constrained to deceive because of a combination of
two circumstances: his spouse is very beautiful[2] and they are in
foreign parts. He fears that in men's eyes his life will be worth
nothing in comparison with the value they place upon her beauty.
What is life to them will be death to him. Out of expediency and by
means of the deception involving his legal relationship to a woman,
the patriarch acts as he does.

Some scholars suggest that the three-fold telling of such an
incident becomes more intelligible in light of a legal practice
favoured by the upper class members of a society, the Hurrian,
which in time and place is linked to patriarchal.[3] In making a
woman a wife, a member of this group also made her, by a legal
fiction, his sister. The suggestion is that the patriarchs themselves
may have gone in for such status creation. The resulting relationship would be open to misunderstanding, or capable of being used
to one's advantage as in the case of Abraham and Isaac. If any
kernel of historical truth lies along this line of enquiry, the present
narratives in Genesis give little or no hint. It is true that in Genesis
20 Abraham asserts to the foreign king, Abimelech, that Sarah is
both his wife and his (half-) sister.[4] But unlike the Hurrian
examples her sisterly status is a fact (they are the offspring of the
same father) and not a fiction. One can do little or nothing with the
question of the historicity of the accounts. A useful starting point
for any analysis is to ask why the stories have been preserved at all
and in this regard one factor stands out: the appealing element to
any storyteller and his audience of a deception that achieves its
goal but is also laid bare as the action unfolds.[5] The role played by
deceptions in the Genesis narratives is considerable. According to
Eve the serpent beguiled her, and there is also truth in the serpent's
assertion that God had deceived Adam and Eve about the fatal
nature of the tree in the middle of the garden. A series of recipro-
cated deceptions is found in the multi-faceted material relating to

Jacob, Esau and Laban. Simeon and Levi trick Shechem and his father Hamor in order to avenge the wrong done to their sister Dinah. The role of deception at different points in the Joseph story is well known. Tamar achieves her goal of obtaining a child by a ruse perpetrated on Judah.

By his duplicity Abraham successfully avoids his own death and, receiving largesse on account of Sarah's great appeal, is aggrandised in the process. The story, originally, was probably intended to extol the successful Abraham. Over a period of time, however, the deception and its consequences became subject to increasing moral reflection and it is during this process that the existing narratives in Genesis have emerged. With the construction of certain biblical laws inspired by them the process was further advanced.

Moral sensitivity in the three narratives is centred on the issue of the matriarch's virtue. In Genesis 12 divine disfavour falls upon the Pharaoh's action in taking a man's wife – an action that constitutes an unwitting trespass on his part because of Abram's deception. The plague that strikes, however, is solely directed against the Pharaoh and his house, which at this point will include Sarai, and which, like the plague in Genesis 20, probably impairs the fertility of the women in the house. Abram's moral role in the affair, although central from the point of view of the Pharaoh who rebukes him for it, is not brought up in any other way.[6]

In Genesis 20 sensitivity about Sarah's virtue reaches a stage in which the writer of the narrative introduces a manifestly contrived event, a dream, that succeeds in rescuing her honour and saving her from a union that he would consider demeaning to her. The situation of Abraham and Sarah (their names having been modified) is very similar to that in Genesis 12. They are again in foreign parts, in Abimelech's kingdom of Gerar. He, having been made to think that she is Abraham's sister, takes her in good faith into his house. One night – so we are to believe – Abimelech learns in a dream that Sarah is Abraham's wife, he refrains from touching her, her virtue remains untarnished, and she is restored to Abraham. The motivation for this contrived element is undoubtedly the feeling of the narrator that it is intolerable for him and his group to believe that their ancestral mother could have been treated so cheaply. As a result the story has a quite different outcome from that in Genesis 12: in the latter her virtue is definitely compromised; here it is rescued, in an albeit roundabout, dramatic last minute fashion.

The third, brief, and final story in Genesis 26 involving Isaac and Rebecca at the court of Abimelech is interesting in one respect only. The near miss that Sarah experienced in Genesis 20 is remote in the case of Rebecca. Much less dramatically than in Sarah's situation, and more realistically, Rebecca is seen by Abimelech in the arms of Isaac, and the deception that she is his sister is found out before Abimelech or one of his court becomes involved with her. In a sense, and especially when thought of in relation to the two other stories, this one stops short, or has been made to stop short. The point is made by Abimelech that, because of Isaac's deception in making it out that Rebecca was his sister, someone *might* have lain with her and brought guilt upon his group. Abimelech would not want that to happen, he is a morally upright man, and he issues the stern warning: 'Whoever touches this man or his wife shall be put to death.'[7]

The moral sensitivity of varying degree that underlies all three stories did not cease with their compilation in the book of Genesis. The problem raised by the patriarch's deception in compromising his wife's virtue received more intense and critical reflection from the Deuteronomic lawgiver. By this time a certain group attitude, in effect an Israelite national consciousness with its interest in how Israelites should behave with, or in contrast to, outsiders as well as with one another,[8] could not accept the compromising conduct on the part of the patriarchs. The account of it was didactically suspect, especially so if the problem of their lack of legal status in foreign parts was ignored, and was no model for the idealised Israelite nation addressed in Deuteronomy. The result was the construction of a law unique in the annals of legal literature. That law prohibits a man from seeking to have his wife restored to him after he has divorced her and she has been taken by another man, who in turn has died or divorced her.[9] The law owes its existence entirely to the Deuteronomist's critical reflection on the patriarchal case. Abram, by requesting Sarai to say that she was his sister, in a way changed her status as his wife with the result that she became another man's wife. As the story in Genesis 12 relates, the second husband, the Pharaoh, was compelled by the deity under threat of death by plague to release Sarai, and she in turn was restored to Abram. The Deuteronomist is not only opposed to what took place in this particular account, but his response has led him to construct his unique law.[10]

It is, after all, a puzzle why the law prohibits the renovation of a marriage after the woman has been released by a second husband because he dislikes her or because he dies. Should the first husband seek her back, the law refers to a woman in this position as being defiled (*tame'*). In what sense is she defiled? Only in that she is going back to her first husband after having been, legitimately, with another man. She would not be defiled in proceeding to a third union because of her second husband's disliking her and divorcing her. If we press – why then is she defiled in taking up marriage again with her first husband – there can be no satisfactory explanation if we isolate the construction of the law from its connection with the historical traditions in Genesis. Only the moral repugnance on the part of the lawgiver to what happened to Sarai because of Abram's manipulation of her can account for the reference in the law to the woman's defilement.

Abram let his marital bond with Sarai be broken because he anticipated that disassociating himself from her in this way would lead to his preservation. For him the danger was occasioned by his wife's great beauty; in particular, the exposure of it to other eyes signalled potential disaster for him. On account of this 'nakedness of a thing' (*'erwat dabar*), that is, something visible that in the nature of things he is unable to cover up, and which occasions difficulties because he is on foreign territory,[11] Abram chose to let Sarai go. I state the matter in this way in order to illumine the difficult expression, 'the nakedness of a thing', used in the law in reference to the reason why the husband chooses to divorce his wife.

As commentators have pointed out, it is difficult to read much or any moral content into this expression, because the same one is used in the law in Deut 23:15(14) without any moral basis: with reference to the problem of what the eyes see, in this instance the deity's sensitivity to the sight of faeces in the Israelite military camp.[12] Sarai's physical appearance in foreign parts constitutes from Abram's point of view a classic instance of what other eyes might see,[13] and hence the apparently vague expression in the law also becomes more intelligible in the light of this background. If the Deuteronomist intended the law to apply to a more conventional situation in his time, we would have to reckon with reasons for divorce such as how a man's wife comported herself in the eyes of others;[14] which in real life very much means how her public conduct was viewed in his eyes. As the law states, 'When a man takes a wife, and marries her, if then she finds no favour in his eyes because he has found the nakedness of a thing in her . . .' To paraphrase, perhaps too narrowly, he finds something in her which proves troublesome to him because of the situation in which he is placed. The neutral nature of the expression, 'the nakedness of a thing', must not be forgotten. It must not be taken to imply anything immoral in her actual conduct. The law's negative formulation, which has understandably encouraged a bad connotation to be read into this expression, is attributable to the fact that a divorce is taking place. A husband's proceeding in this formal manner is inevitably interpreted as involving a totally negative attitude towards the woman. In this particular instance it is important for the husband to convey that impression because the outside world is not meant to know what is truly going on. The law is largely formulated from an outsider's view of things.

Another way to appreciate the connection between the law and the tradition is to note the narrow scope of the law, and to puzzle over what motivates such narrowness. The law confines itself to a situation that must have been relatively rare. That, in addition, there existed in the Deuteronomist's time a real-life problem in a man's divorcing a woman, her marriage to another and a subsequent dissolution of this bond, to be followed by a re-marriage to the first husband, is improbable.[15] On the face of it, it does not seem likely that the lawgiver is concerned to have a man think seriously, before divorcing a woman, whether or not he might regret his decision and seek to have her back. Doubtless, if she remained single he could renew the marriage. The problem is that, in the interval between the divorce and his desire to have her back, she has put a second husband through her hands. It is quite unreal to expect a man who is about to divorce a woman to take such reckoning about her future into account.[16]

Yet in thinking about the law in isolation one is compelled to consider such a possibility as giving rise to it. In the end the only plausible explanation is that the lawgiver is responding to a situation known to him in which a man resorted to divorce, or to an action tantamount to it, not because he really wished to put his wife away,[17] but because he found it expedient to do so. She then left him, took up residence with another man, who himself let her go, and the first husband was faced with what happened to be a pleasant prospect for him,[18] a re-union with her. We are led, not to a contemporary problem at the time of legislation, but to the exceptional circumstances of Abraham's problem (and Isaac's): his possession in a foreign land of a beautiful wife and his fear that a powerful man would desire her; in fact did so and took her into his home.

The circumstances implied in the law are different from those described in the Genesis traditions in so far as the legislator has transposed them into the context of the Israelite homeland and shed them of their idiosyncrasy. Moreover, in that his interests are legal and national, he formulates, as he sees it, the main matter that requires attention – the question whether an Israelite motivated by expediency can divorce a wife so that another man can have her, and possibly still expect at some opportune time to get her back again. The legislator cannot oppose the man's action – Yaron is right to infer that this law presupposes that a man need not show cause for divorce[19] – but he dislikes it because dishonour of the woman is involved. What he can oppose is any hope that he may get her back again. Hence he rules out any renovation of the marriage should the woman become free again, either because she is again divorced or because the second husband dies. If the expression 'the nakedness of a thing' refers to something immoral which accounts for the first divorce, then if the man need not give any reason for divorcing the woman, we are left wondering why this unexceptional, perfectly acceptable one is stated in the law. If, however, his reason is the quite exceptional, shocking one of expediency, an indication of his motivation in the law's formulation is important; because the lawgiver is going to find it unacceptable in the context of his wishing her back at some future point.

We can now say that what prompts the law is the problem thrown up by the Genesis traditions, and in fact the concern to have a man think twice before divorcing a woman should expediency be the motive, and should this involve her becoming the wife of another man. In these circumstances, where the first husband knows that a second husband is likely to be available and waiting, it is not so strange to ask a man to realise that he will lose her for all time, and therefore, to reconsider. The narrowness of the law stands out and becomes more intelligible on this basis.[20]

Some internal evidence from the law lends support to the above analysis. The description of the first divorce is different from that of the second. In the latter the language does not admit of any doubt that the second husband wishes to be rid of her – he dislikes her. In the former the language is not, or is only indirectly, descriptive of the husband's personal feelings. She has not found favour in his eyes because 'he has found in her the nakedness of a thing', that is, not some blemish in her, but quite the reverse, only not the thing in itself, but in a social context;[21] something that cannot be concealed, that, presumably, invites or is likely to invite the longing eyes of another man, and that causes the husband, for whatever reason, to bow to the pressure. It makes no sense to infer some indecency (RSV), something shameful (NEB), as that which the man finds in the woman. It is likely that the Deuteronomist would treat such a fault very severely – recall the fate of the disobedient son, or the fate of the girl who is found guilty of harlotry. Moreover, if the man put her away the first time because of some moral blemish or shameful attribute, it is difficult to understand why he would desire to have her back should she become free after another marriage. One is also left wondering why the second husband was attracted to her.

The law's construction cannot be understood without recourse to reflection on the patriarchs' situation. That is why one should not look initially for some pressing, realistic, recurring problem in a conventional setting. Moreover, the link with the tradition explains why the law does not explicitly say that the first husband divorces his wife because of the attentions she is receiving from another man. Abraham and Isaac's actions were in anticipation only of such a response. The change of status that they conferred upon their wives was before another male actually appeared upon the scene. The law too concentrates on the first husband's action in regard to his wife and does not state explicitly any connection between this action and the appearance of a second husband. It might be noted, however, that some of the details in the law's formulation can be taken to suggest that the woman goes immediately from one husband to the next. She departs from her first husband's house and goes and becomes another man's wife. The RSV has added, what is not in the text, 'And if she becomes another man's wife'. That 'if' is intended to convey a lapse of time between one marriage and the next in such a way as to deny any connection there might be between her going from one husband to the next. Its addition is wholly unwarranted and reveals the difficulties interpreters have with the law. A literal translation of it is:

> If a man takes a woman and marries her, and it shall be that if she does not find favour in his eyes because he has found in her the nakedness of a thing, and he writes her a bill of divorce and puts it in her hand and sends her out of his house, and she departs from his house and goes and becomes another man's

[wife]. And the latter husband dislikes her and writes her a
bill of divorce and puts it in her hand and sends her out of his
house or the latter husband dies, who took her to be his wife,
her former husband who sent her away cannot marry her, to
return to take her to be his wife after she has been defiled; for
that is an abomination before the Lord and thou must not
cause the land to sin which the Lord thy God gives thee as an
inheritance.

A modern analogy to the kind of issue raised in this remarkable
law might be sought in the use of a bribe to gain some favour from
someone. One man pays the other the bribe and the latter fails to
carry out the favour. The man then seeks his money back. The
judgment of a court would be that both parties knew they were
doing wrong and it would let matters stand. In other words, the
man would not receive his money back. Just so, in speculating about
how the Deuteronomist could have viewed the application of his
law in a contemporary setting, we have to imagine that the first
husband divorces his wife so that another can have her in return
for some favour. Should this favour not be forthcoming, and even
should it have been rendered, the second husband might decide to
hold on to the woman even though he had agreed to divorce her
after a certain period of time. The judgment of the law would be
that both parties had acted wrongfully and it would let the matter
stand. It would, however, go a step further. Should the second
husband eventually divorce her, or should he die, it would prohibit
the first husband's marrying her again.

A man's hating a woman is the ordinary reason why a divorce
takes place. Again it might seem puzzling why, if no reason for a
divorce need be given, the ordinary one is stated in the case of the
second husband. This puzzle disappears once it is recognised that
the lawgiver is removing *any* prospect of the first husband's taking
her back again. In the situation contemplated in the possible
application of the law, the second husband would probably proceed
to divorce her on grounds not having to do with his personal
feelings, but because of the bargain struck with the first husband.
Should he so act the lawgiver would prohibit the first husband from
receiving her back. Such a decision can occasion no surprise; in
fact it is so obvious that there would be no need to state it. The lawgiver has to go further. He has to anticipate the not unlikely
development where devious wrongdoers are concerned that the
second husband might decide to hold on to her, and then find him-

self in the situation usual with divorce of disliking the woman. Should that happen his release of her at this point would still not permit the first husband to marry her again. This typical situation, plus the additional one of the man's death would, in so far as the lawgiver is taking into account all of the circumstances likely to arise, become the important ones, because they are the two standard possibilities which might provide the opportunity for the first husband to get his wife back again.

In judging whether this kind of situation was conceivable in the Deuteronomist's time, two factors suggest that while no doubt it would be exceptional, it could occur. First, as we already noted, there was no requirement to declare why a divorce was taking place[22] and, secondly, sexual attitudes would have been much looser in those times. A piece of evidence in support of the latter point is that the Deuteronomist's austere sexual morality will be a reaction to its opposite, the absence of standards in his contemporary setting.[23]

In Genesis the patriarch was treated well on account of his wife's entry into another man's house.[24] The issue of the first husband's gaining favour by releasing his wife is thus easily derived from the traditions. The lawgiver's objection to such exploitation of a woman has already come out in a preceding rule in his code,[25] in his reform of an earlier law in the *Mishpatim*.[26] That law permits a father to refuse his daughter to her seducer. By refusing, he still collects the marriage price for virgins and is able to obtain an additional brideprice from another man. In his law the Deuteronomist denies a father a right of refusal, thereby closing this loophole, because he does not wish a woman to be the means by which, in this instance, a father is enriched.[27]

We can be even more precise in stating why the lawgiver presents his law prohibiting the renovation of a marriage. The reason has to do with the reshaping that has gone into the narrative of Genesis 20 and its effect on him. That narrative, we noted, is motivated by a desire to avoid Sarah's virtue being cheapened in the manner related in Genesis 12. There are indications that an original version told how Sarah was taken by Abimelech in the same way as she was taken by the Pharaoh in Genesis 12. First and foremost is the strain on our credulity that Abimelech realised during the night in a dream that the man's sister whom he had taken (and who doubtless was lying at his side) was in fact the man's wife. God's coming to Abimelech in the dream smacks of an attempt to preserve appearances for Sarah's sake. In fact, this concern with the vindication of Sarah's honour is brought out later in the narrative, when Abimelech tells Sarah that he has given a thousand pieces of silver to her brother as a 'covering of the eyes' to all her acquaintances.[28] If we follow the direction of the existing narrative this statement is supposed to mean that Abimelech had no conjugal tie with Sarah. The fact that payment is given, however, suggests that he had relations with her but in the belief that she was the man's sister. In this light the offence to Sarah is covered over, as is Abraham's deception, by appeal to an overstrict legal interpretation of Sarah's relationship to Abraham: she is in fact his sister. Another indication that an original version was much more straightforward than the present one is seen in God's pronouncement of the death sentence upon Abimelech: 'Behold, thou art a dead man because of the woman which thou hast taken, for she is a man's wife.' So the deed has been done. A few verses later, however, we are to learn that the deity knows Abimelech had not touched Sarah. The contradiction can only be resolved on the basis of a reworked version.

Not only has an original story been changed in the interests of the mother of the nation, but it has also been changed in the interests of having Abraham appear in a better light. No longer in the narrative in Genesis 20 is it recorded that Abraham's problem with his wife is her great beauty. Instead it is baldly stated: 'And Abraham said of Sarah his wife, "She is my sister".' Unlike the narrative in Genesis 12 (and in Genesis 26), no motive for his deception is provided. Indeed, it becomes clear, when Abimelech demands an explanation from Abraham about Sarah's status, that the author intends Abraham to appear justified in saying that she was his sister.

As the narrative in Genesis 20 stands now the requirements of the Deuteronomic law would not rule out the restoration of Sarah to Abraham after her time with Abimelech. She had not been taken sexually by him. The point is, however, that it is precisely the outcome to be found in the existing account of Genesis 20 that motivates the legislator to state his law. This version is something of a *tour de force*. One question it raises is: what if God had not intervened and Sarah had become Abimelech's wife? The Deuteronomist, we shall find, frequently asks of a situation in a tradition: how should it be dealt with in the unremarkable circumstances where the deity does not intervene? Moreover, because of his strict sexual morality and his concern for a woman's honour, the lawgiver is taken up with the question of Sarah's going from one man to the next and then back to the first. Such treatment of her is repugnant to him. The deity's intervention, even though it is motivated by similar repugnance, is apt to confuse what is going on at the human level. It is in response to this possible confusion in the minds of later hearers of the tradition that the law is given.

Noteworthy in respect of the law's formulation is the very careful, clear-cut, and detailed statements concerning the separation of the woman from the second husband. 'And the latter husband dislikes her and writes her a bill of divorce and puts it into her hand and sends her from his house, or the latter husband dies who had taken her to be his wife.' Such language may reflect a concern with practical aspects of divorce, but it can also be seen to reflect the lawgiver's care in spelling out, by way of contrasting Abimelech's relationship to Sarah, that the second husband had taken her as his wife. Similar considerations apply to the initial part of the law. Later hearers of the tradition about Abraham's action in regard to his wife would be confused about what exactly it amounts to in a less dramatic situation. The lawgiver decides to spell out such a situation in terms of a formal divorce.

This concern to clarify any obscurity in later thinking about a problem like Abraham's explains why the law even bothers to detail procedure in the case of a man's putting away his wife. Note that the use of a bill of divorce is taken for granted in the law. If the recipients of the law know about such documents why is it necessary to relay the various steps involved in a divorce? Surely a description of these can be dispensed with. Why not simply a statement such as, 'If a man puts away his wife, and she becomes another man's wife and he in turn puts her away, or he dies . . . ?' No need, as Yaron thinks,[29] to spell things out because a woman who does not receive a bill of divorce might find herself later accused of adultery. The unnecessary detailing of how the divorce takes place is prompted by the need for clarification when reflecting upon a situation such as Abraham's. It is difficult to describe what he was doing with Sarah and it is also difficult to explain, if viewed from the human perspective, Abimelech's release of her. The task is simplified from the legal point of view by restating the problem that came up there because of the deity's interference in terms of a double marriage and a double divorce for the woman.

The link between the later lawgiver's concerns and the Genesis traditions comes out in common language and common ideas. The phrase a man's wife (*be'ulat ba'al*) in Gen 20:3 is the technical expression employed in the Deuteronomic law on adultery.[30] It is not found elsewhere in biblical material. We shall in fact see that this adultery law has been constructed because, in looking at the matter legally, Sarah's role in events in Genesis 20 demands clarification.[31] The word 'covering' in the expression 'a covering of the eyes' (*kesut 'enayim*) has in regard to Sarah's virtue a sexual connotation analogous to that intended in the Deuteronomic law concerning the tassels an Israelite should attach to the corner of his garment or covering (*kesut*). The tassels serve to remind an Israelite to avoid letting his eyes seek illicit sexual encounters; to restrain him from uncovering himself in a wanton way.[32] Abimelech claimed on behalf of Sarah (and on his own behalf) that there was no wanton disregard of her honour. This concern with maintaining a good impression for her among her acquaintances is a feature of the reworked Genesis narrative. Sensitivity to preserving appearances is a predominant feature of the Deuteronomic legislation.[33]

The view that the fear of God (*Elohim*) should be a universal feeling and not just confined to the group (Abraham, Isaac, Jacob and their descendants), whose allegiance is to *Elohim*, is common to the narrative and a Deuteronomic law. Abraham thought that the foreigner, Abimelech, would not show it and the Deuteronomist condemns the foreigner, Amalek, for failing to show it.[34]

Abimelech roundly rebuked Abraham for his whole conduct and claimed that it caused a great sin to come upon not just himself but also his kingdom. This view that the entire land is affected by an offence is a major theme of Deuteronomy. For example, any man who renovates his marriage after the woman has been through another marriage, which he had encouraged her to enter in the first place, causes the land to sin.

In the narrative a powerful idea and one central to its final orientation is that no matter how deceived by circumstances a man might be, so long as he is well intentioned providence will keep him from committing an offence. Abimelech, deceived into thinking that Sarah was a free woman when in fact she was a man's wife, was kept from an adulterous union by the deity because the latter acknowledged his upright character. This profound belief in the providential governance of human conduct is also found throughout Deuteronomy. If a man is right thinking and obedient to the commandments of the Mosaic law God will direct his way in a most beneficial manner.[35]

The spirit that motivates the final shape of the narrative in Genesis 20 has also inspired the law in that both narrative and law react against the situation of Sarai in Egypt, when the second husband enjoyed a union with her. The latter tradition does indeed contain a negative attitude to what took place. It is, however, less specific in its orientation toward Sarai's honour. If we turn to the narrative in Genesis 26 in which a situation similar to Genesis 20 does not reach the stage attained in the latter, an interesting link between this 'non'-story and the law can be made.

The third story, in which no untoward development took place, tells how Isaac's decision to pass his wife off as his sister was vitiated because he was found out. Rebecca does not leave her husband's side and is 'prevented' from doing so because Abimelech happens to see that they really are husband and wife.[36] It is perhaps implied that, as in his dealings with Sarah in Genesis 20, Abimelech had again been directed by God in the matter. In any case, as the story now reads concentration falls upon Isaac's initial ploy.

The lawgiver primarily addresses himself to the fundamental problem that was the root cause of all that took place in Genesis: the initial decision by the patriarch to pass his wife off as his sister. This is the one common element in the three narratives. As a reaction to this situation the lawgiver wants a man to consider at the outset the circumstances which prompt him to divorce a wife and what the consequences might be: dismiss her and he might find that he is not permitted to have her back should she become free again after a second marriage. The lawgiver's focus on what takes place at the beginning of things has as a precedent the strange non-development of the story in Genesis 26. The result is that the trend discernible in the three Genesis narratives has been taken further by the lawgiver.

One final point about the law has to be made. The interpretation given above has claimed that the lawgiver, in taking up from the ancient tradition, has directed his attention toward a possible contemporary situation which concerns a shocking action involving two men. There is no problem in seeing why most of the lawgiver's attention is concentrated on the first husband and his action, and why he tends to describe the situation largely in terms of outward appearances. What remains problematic is the lack of explicitness in stating what is going on between the two men. I have argued that this lack stems in part from the case where Abraham, for example, did not enter into negotiations with Abimelech about Sarah. He simply anticipated the development and was proved correct. We might say that so sure was he of what would take place that he reckoned there was no need for a discussion to work out a deal. He set things up so that his favour followed automatically.

But another reason for the lack of explicitness may well be the intention of the lawgiver not to draw overmuch, or even any, attention to the source of inspiration for his law. To have done so might have proved disturbing to many of his contemporaries. It is one thing to have a tradition about a great ancestor whose life is full of the most tremendous, life-threatening, and momentous occurrences. The utterly exceptional character of his circumstances injects a legendary element into them, and puts him on a plane that prevents people looking too closely at their down-to-earth, real-life aspect. It is quite another thing for someone, such as the Deuteronomist, to come along and look at matters in precisely this way. The results are frequently shown to be disturbing. We shall have occasion to observe that this lawgiver is indeed sensitive to such matters and has, in regard to some of them, a means of communicating which conceals for those who might be offended, and reveals for those who can handle the criticism of their venerable ancestors.

SARAH, RACHEL, LEAH, AND DINAH

From the viewpoint of Abram (Abraham) and Isaac their initial
difficulty when they entered foreign territory that they presumed
to be generally hostile was anticipating the effects of their wives'
beauty upon the inhabitants. The expected awkwardness prompted
their decision to pass them off as their sisters. This decision in turn
encouraged the development that took place: the native king's
desire for a foreign woman and the ensuing problem of, for example,
Abimelech's relationship to Sarah because of the confusion surrounding her status, that is, whether or not she was still Abraham's
wife. Central to the concern of this particular tradition is the dishonour of the woman, Sarah.

The proverbial nature of the Deuteronomic laws is a marked
characteristic:[1] they are interested in matters which, in their
essential features, come up again and again in human affairs. For
the Deuteronomist the ancient experiences of his ancestors constitute an especial interest. It is therefore worth noting that
Abimelech's appropriation of the foreign woman, Sarah, is not an
isolated happening from this period of history. She had already
undergone a similar one with the Pharaoh.[2] Rebecca, too, had been
put at risk in a foreign court.[3] Dinah, Jacob's daughter, was
humbled, wrongfully taken, in foreign parts by the Hivite,
Shechem.[4] Laban reproached Jacob, when the latter acted to return
to his own home and country, for appropriating his daughters 'like
captives of the sword'.[5] That each of these ancestresses had something unusual occur in connection with a marital situation that
also involved an international problem is remarkable. Their
common experience has not escaped the attention of the Deuteronomist.

This lawgiver, addressing his laws to the Israelites, takes up the
topic of a man's desire for a foreign woman and his proper treatment
of her. Only he does so in terms of a situation that might confront
the Israelites. From the viewpoint of their experience the parallel is
one, and it is all the closer because of the element of hostility present
in each of the Genesis traditions,[6] that is most likely to be met when

they are engaged in warfare in foreign parts; when one of them sees a foreign woman and desires to have her. Hence the law in Deut 21:10–14:

> When thou goest forth to war against thine enemies, and the Lord thy God gives them into thine hands, and thou takest them captive, and seest among the captives a beautiful woman,[7] and thou hast desire for her and wouldest take her for thyself as wife, then thou shalt bring her home to thine house, and she shall shave her head and pare her nails. And she shall put off her captive's garb, and shall remain in thine house and bewail her father and her mother a full month; after that thou mayest go into her, and be her husband, and she shall be thy wife. Then, if thou hast no delight in her, thou shalt let her go where she will; but thou shalt not sell her for money, thou shalt not treat her as a slave, since thou hast humiliated her.

The remarkable and completely puzzling reference to a *beautiful* woman in what is supposedly a sober piece of legislation can now be explained. This non-legal, extravagant language betrays the origin of the law in the lawgiver's interest in the beautiful patriarchal wives.[8] Understandably, the lawgiver could not seek to legislate for one of their situations: the problem, intensified by their attractiveness, which confronts men's wives when they are taken to a foreign country.[9] More realistically, and legislatively possible, his concern is with a woman taken captive abroad during a military campaign and brought back to the Israelite homeland. Abraham and Sarah, for example, were on foreign territory because of famine in their own country and not because of capture in war. Nonetheless, Abraham feared for his life. He reckoned that he might well be treated as an enemy and that Sarah would be regarded as a captive. In that her position as a patriarchal wife would be an important one in Israelite tradition, and in that her treatment on alien territory invited critical scrutiny, the lawgiver is all the more ready to counsel Israelites on the proper way to treat a foreign captive woman.[10] This central concern with the treatment of a woman who is away from her own family and country is the primary link between the law and this particular tradition.

There is no reference to Sarah's beauty in Genesis 20. Its omission is to be attributed to the attempt of the redactor of this version to make the patriarch seem less obviously deceptive than in the other two stories. In them the patriarch's concentration on his wife's beauty leads to the strategy of making her out to be his sister. In Genesis 20 we hear of no conversation between Abraham and Sarah in which they agree to the subterfuge. Rather, it is simply reported that in Gerar Abraham said of Sarah, 'She is my sister', and this version goes on, unlike the one in Genesis 12, to make much of the fact that she is indeed a (half-) sister. Later surveyors of this tradition, such as the Deuteronomist, would still have raised questions about all of the reasons for Abraham's actions, and readily aligned them with those found in the other two traditions.

In many instances, we shall see, the language used in the later laws comes directly from the Genesis material. For example, the phrase 'beautiful in form' is taken, not from the words of the patriarch in Gen 12:11, 'I know that thou art a woman beautiful to behold', nor from Gen 26:8, 'because she was fair to look upon', but from the description of Jacob's loved wife, Rachel, in Gen 29:17. Apart from the identical phrase (y^e *pat-to' ar*) – only found in the Pentateuch in these two places in reference to women[11] – the very next law in Deut 21:15–17 about the loved and the hated wife has focused on the tradition about Rachel and Leah.[12]

One reason for borrowing the phrase from the application to Rachel is that she is the original Israel's wife, and the law is concerned with a woman who is to become the wife of a son of Israel. Another and more powerful reason is that part of the Jacob tradition has it that Rachel herself was carried off by Jacob as a captive. Thus the original Israel on the way to his homeland was overtaken by Laban, the father of Rachel and Leah, and asked, 'What hast thou done, that thou has cheated me, and carried away my daughters like captives of the sword?' Laban goes on to tell him that he should have observed proper procedure in taking Rachel and Leah from their ancestral home. The fact that Jacob's joint marriage to the two sisters occupies the attention of the law following the one about the captive woman is a strong indication that his action is very much in mind also in the law about her. This tradition about Jacob's acquisition of his wives would tie in with the concern the lawgiver had about Sarah's situation.

In commenting on the Genesis incident involving Jacob's flight from Laban, David Daube writes, 'In the background is a law like that in Deuteronomy which envisages marriage with a captive woman without the usual preliminaries. Jacob, Laban complains, chose this sort of marriage; whereas Laban would have preferred the friendly, ceremonious, legal one, seeing them off "with mirth and songs, with timbrel and harp".[13] The latter language alludes to wedding festivities – so Jer 7:34, 16:9, 25:10. Daube sees the connection between the law and the tradition as one in which an earlier law or usage approximated the one preserved in Deuteronomy. This is correct but we can be more specific and say that the earlier usage would not have existed in a written form in the Deuteronomist's time,[14] and that he was spurred to a statement of what the law should be in regard to his own time precisely because Laban's complaint was by way of an analogy only to the capture of women in war. Clarification is required of how an Israelite, a son of Jacob, should proceed in the matter of appropriating a female captive. The Laban incident raises the topic but Jacob was already married to Rachel and Leah. His marriage to them, especially his union with Leah, raised their own questions, some of which, we shall see, the lawgiver takes up, but the situation was not one of capture in war.

The report of the Laban incident has started the lawgiver in pursuit of his definitive statement about the requirements for an Israelite's taking a woman in capture. To proceed he needed to search further afield, and so he took into consideration the other incidents involving patriarchal wives, and likened them also to the more typical problem of what arises in wartime. For us a consequence of this broader search is that it is more difficult to be precise in working out the connections between the law and the various traditions. Shared language, however, underlines that the links do in fact exist. 'Beautiful in form' (*ye pat-to' ar*), in reference to a woman, only occurs in the Pentateuch in the law and Gen 29:17 (about Rachel), as was noted. 'To delight in' (*ḥašaq*), in the sense of loving a woman, is found only in the law and Gen 34:8 (about Dinah). The synonymous expression 'to take pleasure [in a woman]' (*ḥapeṣ*) is found only in the law, Esther 2:14, and Gen 34:19 (about Dinah). 'To humble' (*'innah*) a woman only occurs in the Pentateuch in Gen 34:2 (about Dinah), in Gen 31:50 (about Rachel and Leah), and in this law, plus the two laws in Deut 22:24, 29 (underlying which Dinah's situation is, as we shall see, very much in the background).

We can readily explain why the language used to describe Shechem's treatment of Dinah is incorporated into the law, even though the two situations are different. The law, we indicated, is initially inspired by Laban's likening Jacob's removal of his daughters from their homeland to the capture of females in war.

For the purpose of constructing a law on the subject the lawgiver has in turn likened Abimelech's taking Sarah and Shechem's taking Dinah to such capture. It so happens that Shechem's deed, in terms of actually taking a woman, is closest to the kind of situation that is likely to arise in acquiring a woman in war. Hence the language used to describe what he did can be usefully transferred to matters pertinent to that event and its subsequent development: the Israelite warrior delights in the foreign female, acquires her, ceases to take pleasure in her, rids himself of her, and in doing so must be reminded that he had already humbled her because of his initial appropriation without a father's consent.

In keeping with his strict sexual morality on the one hand and his related concern with a woman's honour on the other, the Deuteronomist prohibits contact with the woman until a month is passed. During this period she has to show proper respect for her parents, which respect will or should enhance her own honour in the eyes of an Israelite. Moreover, she has to alter her outward appearance by paring her nails and shaving her head. Such a concern with appearances is characteristic of the strong shame-cultural bias in Deuteronomy. But whatever other reasons lie behind the directions,[15] one of them might well stem from the Deuteronomist's response to the situations described in Genesis. In those narratives the woman's physical appeal is a feature that is openly stated in Genesis 12 and 26, and the impression of a male's haste to enjoy her is suggested.[16] Conceivably, the Deuteronomist has reacted in the interests of upholding the worth of the woman as not being dependent upon her physical attractiveness. Moreover, he rules out haste by insisting upon a period of one month elapsing before the marriage is consummated. The traditions concerning Rachel and Dinah also suggest that this factor might be under consideration. In Gen 29:9–30 Jacob waited, or was made to wait, a month before he declared, or could declare, his desire for Rachel. Remarkably, he then had to wait seven years before he could marry her. They passed quickly, he felt, but the whole episode raises pointed questions about what constitutes reasonable procedure in such matters. Shechem, on the other hand, proceeded with indecent haste in appropriating Dinah. In the aftermath of his action there was an attempt to make his appropriation of her more acceptable. Again the factor of haste to enjoy her emerges. In becoming circumcised he 'did not delay to do the thing, because he had delight in Jacob's daughter'.[17]

Another indication of the traditions' influence on the construction of the law is to be observed in the latter's concern that the union might not work out. Contracting a marriage and dissolving it are two separate legal topics, yet the two matters are raised together in the one law. This feature can be explained by noting that reflection upon the narrative of Genesis 20, for example, would readily entail a joint treatment of the two issues. Abimelech almost contracted a union with Sarah; in fact the narrative, as we noted, appears to have reshaped the original facts which did tell of an actual one. Abimelech, in turn, had to undo his relationship with her and pay her brother, Abraham, a sum of money by way of upholding her honour in the eyes of others. To be sure, as the story now reads, this action is not the equivalent of the dissolution of a marriage with Sarah. It is more an affirmation that some kind of sexual relationship between them was thought to exist and required a formal acknowledgment that it had not really existed. Nonetheless, for Deuteronomic legal purposes it is easy to see how the subject of a man's marrying a foreign woman presented itself and, further, how the question of the breakdown of the marriage also came up.

We must recall how this lawgiver is anxious to break through the obscurities and special circumstances of existing traditions and come up with an issue suitable for his legal constructions. The narrative in Genesis 20 raises the matter of a man's taking a foreign woman and then having to give her up. But the circumstances described are exceptional because of the role of the deity. The narrative about Dinah in Genesis 34 likewise presents an example of a man's taking a foreign woman and her eventual release from his rough-handed appropriation of her. Laban's concern about Jacob's treatment of his two daughters is also pertinent to the specific topic of the dissolution of a marriage. They had been taken like captives, according to Laban. In their subsequent life in Jacob's house, Leah is a wife who never had her husband's favour. A question that readily arises is why Jacob did not put her away, again the kind of issue that would not have escaped the Deuteronomist. Shedding these traditions of their idiosyncratic features, the lawgiver would concentrate his attention on the unremarkable, conventional, parallel situation for an Israelite. That has to be the military one in which the warrior acquires a woman but eventually wishes to be rid of her for the mundane, unexceptional reason that he no longer takes pleasure in her.

The most prominent shared concern of the law and the narratives about Sarah, Dinah, Rachel and Leah is that of the woman's honour. In the law the man must release the woman and let her go where she will, without selling her to anyone. The reason given to justify such a direction is that she has been humbled. In some ways this is a puzzling statement. If we take the law at face value, without regard to any background influence, it is difficult to appreciate the point about the woman's humiliation. Dissolving a marriage is an acceptable procedure and it is therefore surprising that the law does not leave the matter there.[18] But the influence of the narratives has again to be reckoned with. Sarah, for example, was released from the house of Abimelech and permitted to depart unconditionally. The question of payment arose, but in her favour and for the purpose of undoing any humiliation because of her time with Abimelech. This aspect of the narrative might well have prompted the lawgiver to consider the issue of a captive woman's humiliation in the context of a formal divorce.

We can, however, be quite precise in explaining the reference to the humbling of the woman. Daube has argued that it consists in the unceremonious appropriation of her and thus approximates those cases in which the humiliation consists in a man's taking a woman without attending to the correct formalities.[19] Daube concentrates on the way in which she is first acquired, as a captive in war, and he does not view the waiting period before the man may take her sexually as in any way undoing the manner of the initial appropriation. This interpretation would make the man's action very similar to Shechem's. We have already noted that the term 'to humble' is found in this tradition.[20] His humbling Dinah lay in the fact that he had not asked her father about a prospective union with her. In the nature of things the Israelite warrior made no such request of the captive woman's father.

The situation involving Jacob's flight from Laban with his two wives also ties in at this point. After Laban had complained about Jacob's taking them like captives he sought an agreement to the effect that in their subsequent life with him they would not be ill-treated (*'innah*). The term is the same one used to refer to the humbling of Dinah and the captive woman. In particular, Laban demands that Jacob take no wives in addition to Rachel and Leah. The Deuteronomist would readily choose to understand this agreement to mean the kind of thing he lays out in his law. If in the future Jacob sought to be rid of one or both of these wives, he was not, in keeping with his recent action of treating them like captives, to regard them as slaves to be sold. Should a situation of divorce arise, their father, Laban, would not be around to protect their rights. It is easy to see how the lawgiver's reflection upon Laban's agreement with Jacob leads to the topic of protecting a captive woman who might be released from her marriage to an Israelite.

It is well established that the earlier laws of the Book of the Covenant (Ex 21:2–23:19) have received attention in the later Deuteronomic legislation. Exactly in what way the Deuteronomist has reworked them is more complicated.[21] S.R. Driver cites a connection between the restriction imposed on the Israelite (in the Deuteronomic captive woman law) not to sell the woman and the same restriction in Ex 21:8, the case in which a master acquires a man's daughter for the purpose of making her his concubine but in the end does not do so.[22] She can be bought back by her family, or acquired by another Hebrew, but she must not be sold by the man to a foreign people. The captive woman who became an Israelite's wife has no family to redeem her. Moreover, she actually had been taken as a wife before she lost favour in her husband's eyes. In the earlier legislation, if we accept the Massoretic text, as we almost certainly should, the woman had not yet become the man's wife. If she had, and there is a secondary reading to this effect, she would have been released without payment of any money, in accord with the rule in Ex 21:11: failure to uphold her conjugal right entails her release without any compensation to the husband-master. It would appear that the ruling in the Deuteronomic law owes something to this earlier concern with a woman's status. It is noteworthy, for example, that each law is explicitly concerned with the humiliation of the woman, and that she has a low status, a bond-servant in one law, a captive female in the other, a slave, if not for the issue of marriage.

The secondary reading in Ex 21:8, which affirms a master-concubine relationship before his decision to give her up, may well have come into existence because of the Deuteronomist's study of the existing Exodus legislation. In other words, the Deuteronomist was concerned with the more conventional situation in which a man takes a woman and then wishes to release her, but the Exodus law only covered the more exceptional one in which the master intended to marry her, but lost interest before doing so, and decided to regain some of the money he paid in first acquiring her. The question, in the form of the secondary reading ('And if he has acquired her for himself'),²³ was then put in the context of the Exodus legislation, that is, what a master is entitled to if he has had a relationship with her. In reply, the Deuteronomist denies him any payment, a response that would tally with the intent of the rule in Ex 21:11.

A major explanation of why the Deuteronomist's laws differ from earlier laws is because he is perusing them simultaneously with ancient narrative traditions. There is, for example, an un-doubted link between the legislation concerning the release of slaves in Ex 21:2-11 and Deut 15:12-18; but in the latter the explicit citation of the exodus from Egypt indicates the influence of this tradition on the law. A law concerning the theft of a man is found in both Ex 21:16 and Deut 24:7, but in the latter the national emphasis on the theft of a brother Israelite is to be attributed to the Deuteronomist's characteristic reworking of his traditions, in this case the sale of Joseph by his brothers.²⁴ The law of the captive woman is indeed linked to the earlier legislation concerning the treatment of a woman as a wife. The lawgiver has used it, however, in the wider context of his examination of the past traditions of his people. In examining those about Abimelech's dealing with Sarah, Jacob's with Rachel and Leah, and Shechem's with Dinah, he produces his law about the treatment of a foreign woman that is required of an Israelite, should the latter make her his wife and then find themself not willing to continue the marriage. In doing so he used earlier law to guide him in his judgment of what should be done both in situations like those found in the traditions, and also in a parallel, contemporary, more conventional one.

I have argued that there exists a close connection between the Genesis traditions about a patriarch's passing his wife off as his sister and the two laws, the renovation of a marriage and marriage to a captive woman. A casual scrutiny of them readily indicates common features – marriage, the woman's loss of favour, her sub-sequent departure from the man's house, her humiliation – and hence an indication of a shared relationship with the traditions.

LEAH

Jacob had two wives: Rachel, whom he loved but who was barren, and Leah, whom he hated but who was fertile. His first-born son, Reuben, was born to Leah. Eventually Rachel was able to conceive and she bore Joseph. Already in the Genesis narratives there is sympathy for Leah because of her humiliating position as the unloved wife. Compensation consists in her bearing a large number of sons. But even in this area, in one matter, she loses. Jacob's first-born, her son Reuben, does not receive the chief blessing, the prime inheritance, from his father. Instead, the benefit goes to Joseph, the son by the loved wife, Rachel.[1] Admittedly, in Genesis, Reuben's forfeiture of the inheritance is attributed to a serious moral blemish: he lay with Bilhah, his father's concubine.[2] Moreover, Joseph emerges as a very worthy and virtuous son. The fact is, however, that the chief blessing could have gone to a son born before Joseph, for example, to Simeon, Levi, Judah, Issachar, or Zebulon. That Joseph receives it and not Reuben is, therefore, apparently also tied to the love or hate attitude of Jacob toward his wives. The Deuteronomist has read it this way, has concentrated on this aspect of the situation, and he responds to Leah's oppressed position, which is underlined by her offspring's failure to receive the top inheritance, by presenting the law,

> If a man has two wives, the one loved and the other disliked, and they have borne him children, both the loved and the disliked, and if the first-born son is hers that is disliked, then on the day when he assigns his possessions as an inheritance to his sons, he may not treat the son of the loved as the first-born in preference to the son of the disliked, who is the first-born, but he shall acknowledge the first-born, the son of the disliked, by giving him a double portion of all that he has, for he is the first issue of his strength; the right of the first-born is his.[3]

The link between this law and the Genesis tradition is especially clear. The reason for this is again in line with what we have discovered for other laws and other traditions. The narrower the extent of the law the more likely is it to have been inspired by some

singular feature in a tradition. Thus the scope of the inheritance
law, the only one in the Deuteronomic code, is confined to the
unusual, rare case where a man has two wives, one of them is disliked, and she happens to be the one who has produced the first-
born son. Problems of inheritance crop up in much more normal
circumstances than these, for example, among sons of the same
mother. We are led to the question of how certain problems presented themselves to this lawgiver. All the clues point to the
Genesis narratives. Another interesting connection between this
particular law and the Leah tradition stems from observing that in
the law the man appears to be still married to both wives. He has
not, as we might expect, divorced the disliked one.[4] The situation
described in the law reflects Jacob's situation exactly. At no time,
it appears, did he seek to put Leah away.

The fact that Reuben, as the first-fruits of his father's strength
(the figurative language is peculiar to Gen 49:3, in Jacob's farewell
words to Reuben, and to the law), lay with a wife of his father must
constitute an additional motivating factor for the Deuteronomist's
law. Reuben's deed could be seen as obscuring the issue of the
inheritance. Those who knew the tradition would justifiably think
that it was his offence which cut him off from the first-born's share
of the inheritance. What they might not realise, however, is that
even if he had not committed the offence Jacob's favouring Rachel
and their son, Joseph, could have led to the same result. The uncovering of this problem, which might be overlooked, is especially
revealing of the Deuteronomic treatment of ancient tradition.[5]

As in the case of Sarah, so in that of Leah, and as in the two laws,
the captive woman and the renovation of a marriage, the Deuteronomist's sensitivity to the humiliation of women is revealed. The
inheritance law, although apparently intended primarily to
support a first-born son is indirectly concerned with the lot of a
hated wife. On her husband's death she becomes dependent upon
her own sons, and if one of them is the first-born and receives the
greater share of the inheritance, her position is the better secured.

Leah's impact on later biblical law is not exhausted by consideration of the above aspect of the Genesis tradition about her. When
we scrutinise the tradition involving Jacob's daughter, Dinah, we
shall see how the famous wedding night substitution of Leah for
Rachel is directly pertinent to an understanding of that most
puzzling of laws, the husband who slanders his wife immediately
after the consummation of their marriage.[6]

DINAH, LEAH, AND SARAH

Although commonly regarded as one of the most abhorrent narratives in Genesis, the incident involving Jacob's daughter, Dinah, is written up in such a way as to reveal a profound tension of viewpoints between Jacob and his two sons, Simeon and Levi. Equally interesting are the biblical laws that arose from reflection upon the narrative. Two points of view prevail in Genesis 34: Jacob's and someone who takes the side of Simeon and Levi and who is responsible for the present shape of the narrative. In other words, an original story has been reworked – a conclusion shared by most commentators.[1]

Jacob's reaction to his daughter's seduction by Shechem, the Prince of the Hivites, is far removed from the impassioned and angry condemnation of her brothers. His attitude is a calm and cautious one: he looks at the offence in light of the total situation. The attitude is reminiscent of a piece of practical counsel favoured in wisdom circles, 'Good sense makes a man slow to anger, and it is his glory to overlook an offence'.[2] Jacob had held his peace on hearing about the seduction, and Hamor, the head of the Hivites, and he discuss the matter, presumably along the lines of the two groups living together amicably, as outlined in Hamor's later proposals to Jacob's sons.

These sons, and Simeon and Levi in particular, concentrate on the specific offence done to their sister, and they are outraged. The offence constitutes folly from the point of view of their group, Israel; such a thing ought not to have been done. The sons come to terms with Hamor and his group about ways in which the Israelites and the Hivites might live together, but they do so only in order to deceive and to render them vulnerable to attack. The result is the slaughter of Hamor, Shechem, and all their men. Jacob's attitude to things resurfaces: he is disturbed by Simeon and Levi's vengeance on the Hivites. He again looks at the matter as a whole, and fears for the continued safety of his house. The other Canaanites will hear of the slaughter, and the Israelites, being few in number, will invite hostility.[3] The last word, however, lies with Simeon and

Levi and it is about the wrong done to Dinah, 'Should he treat our sister as a harlot?'

While Simeon and Levi have the final word in the narrative, Jacob's last words on the matter are delivered just before he dies.[4] In them he again condemns Simeon and Levi. Characteristic of many of his parting words to his different sons are comparisons of them to animals and, in addition, plays upon words. In the case of Simeon and Levi, Jacob renews his attack on them for their violence to the Hivites. In their anger, he says, they had slain a man and hamstrung an ox. The language is allusive and poetical. A famous man's last words are especially memorable and ancient writers gave them a shape and form appropriate to their legendary quality. To what reality is this particular reference addressed? The man killed is an allusion to the representative head of the Hivites, namely, Hamor. Hebrew poetic parallelism suggests that the second part of the couplet, the hamstringing of the ox, alludes to a related human phenomenon. Jacob had already complained that Simeon and Levi's action in slaughtering Hamor and his men had brought trouble on his own house.[5] He means that his group is few in number and relative to the greater number of the remaining Canaanites it is in a vulnerable position. In effect, Simeon and Levi's action had hamstrung the house of Israel, which in other contexts where a warlike situation exists is compared to an ox.[6]

We can now explain in detail the composition of this allusive couplet. The man slain is Hamor, whose name means Ass. It is a derogatory name and reflects the superior attitude of the Israelites to the Canaanites.[7] The author is saying that Simeon and Levi killed the Ass, and his evocation of the animal reference in the first part of the couplet prompts his reference in the second part to the hamstrung Ox, an allusion to the house of Jacob. Moreover, a wordplay in regard to the hamstringing connects the meaning intended with Jacob's words in Genesis 34:30 about the trouble his house finds itself in because of Simeon and Levi's slaughter of the house of Hamor. The word 'to hamstring' (*'iqqer*) is a play upon 'to trouble' (*'akar*). When Jacob goes on to say that Simeon and Levi will meet with the consequences of their action he continues to use animal imagery. Their offence is that they have threatened Israel with the fate of being swallowed up by the many Canaanites. Their matching punishment, Jacob decrees, is that like animals they will be scattered amidst the larger group, Israel.[8]

The concern of Simeon and Levi with their sister's honour

recalls the strict sexual morality of the wisdom literature, of Joseph in regard to Potiphar's wife (a wisdom narrative), and of Deuteronomy. In the book of Proverbs, for example, the young men addressed are constantly warned about the disastrous consequences of giving way to their sexual passion. The fate of Shechem would serve as an illustration of the negative aspect of this proverbial teaching and Simeon and Levi would stand as living exponents of its positive side. Jacob, on the other hand, would represent the man of experience, not so beset by physical desires and hence not so bothered by them; in other words, one who takes an overall view of matters and proceeds in a practical, expedient manner.[9]

The Deuteronomist's interest in this Genesis tradition is intense. The result is the construction of certain laws that can only continue to puzzle the enquirer who is unaware of their source of inspiration. What is one to make of a prohibition against an ox and an ass ploughing together?[10] In practical terms they are able to plough together and sometimes do. The view that their strength is unequal and that this is the reason for the prohibition conceals more than it reveals,[11] because one would wish to know why a lawgiver was aroused to construct a law on such a trivial subject.

In biblical material similar legislation is sometimes found in two different places. The material similar to the three laws on mixtures in Deut 22:9–11 is in Lev 19:19. Comparison is invited between the breeding of two kinds of cattle and the ploughing of two different animals, the ox and the ass. In fact, once it is realised that 'to plough' can be used figuratively in a sexual sense,[12] the two laws are very close in meaning. The Deuteronomic law uses figurative language (not uncommon for this lawgiver),[13] and its meaning is directed against the ploughing of Dinah, of the house of Israel, the ox, by Shechem, of the house of Hamor, the ass. Elsewhere in Deuteronomy a liaison between an Israelite and a Hivite (the house of Hamor) is forbidden.[14] The prohibition in Deut 22:10 owes its particular cast to the Deuteronomist's interest in Genesis 34. His legislation is addressed to Israel (as a nation) and it is likely that the law represents his critical reaction to the original Israel's noncommittal attitude to his daughter's seduction. 'You [Jacob/Israel] should not plough with an ox and an ass together.' (To repeat. The meaning is figurative. The link to the literal sense is that the animals are doing the ploughing, the person in control having direct or indirect oversight.) The law is intended to leave no doubt in the minds of those who study the narrative in Genesis

34 that Simeon and Levi were right in condemning not just Shechem's taking Dinah in the manner that he did, but also in not permitting connubium between the Israelites and the Hivites, a matter that is raised in the narrative. We again come upon a feature that is a major factor in the origin of the Deuteronomic laws. Doubts in later minds about matters in the traditions, in this instance, Jacob's stance with regard to his daughter's seduction, are taken up and resolved in the laws. Why there is resort to cryptic language in resolving this particular doubt will be considered below.

In going over the Shechem story, the lawgiver, like us, would have no difficulty in noting that, aside from the peculiar initiative of Dinah in sallying forth into foreign terrain, what took place was a consequence of Shechem's giving vent to his passion. Such lack of restraint is a fixed and lively topic of interest among the sages who taught young Israelite men how to conduct themselves wisely. A related topic that also receives attention is the desirability of a young man's acquiring an honourable woman as a wife.

We have seen so far in regard to the Deuteronomic interest in the Genesis material that there is a consistent concern to treat women in a more honourable way. That this concern is linked to wisdom counsel may be seen by noting that a whole series of laws is inspired by the desire of the lawgiver to present at a legal level the sages' warning to avoid wrongful sexual passion. Thus the five laws in Deut 22:13–29 all deal with this topic. The context in which they are unfolded is mainly, but not exclusively, Shechem's treatment of Dinah. That is to say, problems thrown up by this tradition prompt the construction of most of the laws.

In the same section of material as the prohibition against an ox and an ass ploughing together is a law that deals with the case of a man who on marrying a woman makes public statements that she was not a virgin. There are two parts to the law, the first dealing with a disreputable and unfounded attack on the woman's honour and the second with a justified one in which she is condemned as a harlot. It is unlikely that the law represents a juridical response to an actual case of complaint against a new wife: such cases could only be rare. Rather the tradition concerning Shechem's treatment of Dinah posed the primary problem with which the law is concerned, namely, harlotry.

That tradition concludes on a note of outrage, with Simeon and Levi uttering words to the effect that their sister has been treated like a harlot. The Deuteronomist takes up from the narrative at this point. After the Shechem incident Dinah would have returned to her native group. It is easy to appreciate that the lawgiver would raise a question about how she stood in regard to a future marriage within it. Apart from his particular interests, the Genesis material itself touches on the topic of marriage, although not Dinah's, immediately after the events involving Shechem. Jacob's group had been enlarged by the addition of the Hivite women, who were ordered to put away their foreign gods, and change their garments.[15] One reason for the injunction will reflect a concern about the acceptability of these women for marriage to the Israelites.[16] We do not in fact learn anywhere in Genesis about a marriage for Dinah within or outside her group. The matter compels attention. It is just the kind of situation that prompts the Deuteronomist to his legal questions and answers.

The question thrown up by Dinah's status, which is linked to the concern expressed by Simeon and Levi about Shechem's having made her a harlot, has sparked the two-part law in Deut 22:13–21, especially the second part. Part one is concerned with a girl falsely accused of not being a virgin on her wedding night and part two with a girl justifiably accused. If she stands condemned it is because she 'has wrought folly in Israel by playing the harlot in her father's house'. This language is borrowed from Simeon and Levi's condemnation of Shechem. They were angry, 'because he had wrought folly in Israel by lying with Jacob's daughter, for such a thing ought not to be done'.[17]

It is necessary to explain carefully the steps by which the dual subject matter of this law has arisen from a consideration of this Genesis narrative, plus another one yet to be considered. The use of the Genesis traditions for national purposes has to be kept in mind. The lawgiver puts questions to the material in Genesis 34 as if it involved matters Israelite. Shechem's seduction of Dinah raises, as we shall see in the law of Deut 22:28, 29, the issue of an *Israelite's* seduction of an unbetrothed woman. In other words, because Shechem was a Hivite and hence unacceptable to Simeon and Levi (and to the Deuteronomist), the response to his action was different from what it ought to be in the case of an Israelite who acts like him. The Deuteronomic seduction law clarifies the latter situation by putting to the tradition the question: what should be done if an Israelite behaves like Shechem?

To treat a woman in the way that Shechem treated Dinah – to

enjoy her without the formalities of making arrangements with her father or guardian – is to treat her as a harlot. This was the view expressed by Simeon and Levi and the Deuteronomist concurs. Because Shechem did not marry Dinah there is suggested the hypothetical case of a woman who has been seduced before marrying, and who might end up married to another Israelite. He in turn might not know anything about her past affair. This consideration has prompted the second part of the law in Deut 22:13–21: the daughter of Israel who has played the harlot in her father's house, and who, presumably, had no inclination at the time to report her seduction, or the identity of the seducer. It is worth noting in Dinah's case that it was her seducer who, through his father, made contact with her father about the matter. In other words, there is nothing said about Dinah's reporting her seduction.

The first part of the law is inspired by the attempt to produce a case in which an Israelite treats a woman as a harlot in a way other than seducing her when she is unbetrothed. One reason why the lawgiver seeks this additional example is because Shechem did not end up married to Dinah. If an Israelite treats a woman after the fashion of Shechem he would have to marry her, according to the Deuteronomist in his law in 22:28, 29. What then, he asks himself, is another situation in which an Israelite woman might be treated as a harlot? It cannot be any other situation before marriage, but has to be one such as is described in the first part of the law in 22:13–21. Thus one way in which a woman might be so labelled is by her husband's accusing her of past affairs. This first part of the law is particularly concerned with the bad reputation he tries to give her by putting it about that she was not a virgin on her wedding night. Such talk does indeed brand a woman as a harlot.

The girl's parents, according to the law, must take the matter up with the authorities and produce evidence (the stained wedding night garment) that her husband's allegations are baseless and false. He is punished, not on the principle laid down in the law of 19:15–21 that a false charge deserves the punishment (in this case death) of the penalty appropriate to the offence he charged her with, but with a fine, a public whipping, and the permanent responsibility to maintain her as his wife. The lawgiver has not, therefore, concentrated on the fact of the false charge, but on the man's demeaning attack on the woman's virtue. If we concentrate on the legal aspect of the material this change of direction is both remarkable and puzzling. The indirect influence of the Genesis narrative, the dishonourable treatment of Dinah, a daughter of Israel, contributes to this particular bias in the law.

The influence of the Dinah tradition upon the first part of the law is indeed only indirect. Another source of inspiration has to be sought which will account for its particular orientation. The details of the law have to be looked at more closely. Thus the question of what motivates the man's action is a most puzzling feature, the obvious rarity of such an occurrence further underlining the question why the lawgiver comes up with this law in the first place. One possible motivation could be the man's attempt to withdraw from the marriage and recover some of the bride-price.[18] Such a view, however, poses more questions than it answers. Why, for example, did he decide to consummate the union before seeking to break off the relationship ? The puzzle hinges upon an assessment of his action in the immediate aftermath of the wedding night. He would have to make his allegation about her lack of virginity at this time, his case not holding up if he delayed to do so.[19] The question why he chose to slander her rather than simply proceed to divorce her is answered by the fact that divorce so soon after completing the marriage is hardly an option available to him in the normal way of things. A man might not legally need to show cause in order to divorce a woman[20] (hence no need for him to resort to slander), but his standing in the community would require some explanation, especially so if the time between marriage and divorce was so short. Moreover, he would be set back financially by divorcing her and in all likelihood he would be the object of some derision (assuming, of course, that she was a virgin on her wedding night). To repeat, his calumny immediately after the wedding night is the issue that has to be focused on.

What then has prompted the law? The answer is again the Deuteronomist's reflection upon a Genesis tradition. We have seen how features of one tradition often overlap with those of another. This is especially true in matters involving matrimonial incidents. Moreover, in that the laws are addressed to Israel as a nation the traditions involving Jacob-Israel are especially subject to the law-giver's scrutiny. When Jacob on his wedding night was tricked by Laban into taking Leah as his wife he found himself irrevocably bound to her in the morning.[21] It is this incident which has set going the Deuteronomist's reflection and led to the law.

Jacob's situation must have prompted the question among later, and no doubt admiring, hearers of his life and adventures as to what

he should have done in face of Laban's deception. How should he
have retaliated, they might well have asked. The Deuteronomist
would have resisted such hero worship and retrospective urge to
action. Instead, with his moral sobriety and critical instincts, he
would have pondered what a man might be tempted to do by way
of retaliation – for the purpose of countering it, because his concern
would be with the humiliating treatment of the woman. As always,
the ancient story inspires an attempt to present an approximate,
contemporary, less idiosyncratic legal parallel.[22] An alternative way
in which the tradition might have been approached by the Deuteronomist is that he could have noted approvingly how it shows that
Jacob in fact, at least in regard to his union with Leah, did not react
to Laban's roguery. It would then be his concern to bring out the
problem of what could have happened in such a situation, especially
so in that Jacob was given to deception in other matters.

In the law, the man hates (*śane'*) the woman immediately after
he has consummated the union with her. In Gen 29:31, immediately following the information about Laban's tricking Jacob into
a union with Leah, we read: 'The Lord saw that Leah was hated
[*śane'*].'[23] The narrator sees Jacob's hatred of Leah stemming from
his intercourse with her, and the parallel between the law and the
tradition is thus a very precise one. Moreover, we have noted
before how the religious element in a tradition, in this instance,
God's observation of Leah's position, challenges the later lawgiver
to work out the problems involved at the secular, legal level. Jacob's
hatred for Leah would have been primarily directed at her father,
Laban, and it is likely that this factor of anger at the girl's father is
playing a role in the lawgiver's thinking. Noteworthy in this regard
is the puzzling fact that the wedding night cloth is in the possession
of the girl's father and mother, and not in the possession of the
married couple. One reason for this is obviously to safeguard the
woman against the kind of allegation made in the law. Their having
it, however, is also designed to maintain their own respectability,
which, by implication, is also under attack because of the new son-
in-law's action. Should the girl in fact prove to be non-virginal she
is punished at the door of her father's house. Clearly, a stigma
would attach to him if the man's charge is upheld. This development likewise suggests that in the case of a false charge against the
woman the man is also attempting to stigmatise the father.[24]

Basically the law is concerned to deter any male from making a
false allegation of the kind described. Thus should the male try he

will be trapped by the fact of the wedding night garment having been handed over to the girl's father and mother. This evidence will lead to his being chastised, probably by physical means, fined a hundred shekels, a figure double that to be paid to a father whose unbetrothed daughter has been seduced, and required to maintain her as a wife all his days. The most likely, *specific* factor that has prompted the law is the Deuteronomist's observation that Jacob, when he might have been expected to, did not resort to any deception when he was cheated into taking Leah. Even though Laban's action resulted in Jacob's hatred of Leah he did not at any time in the future seek to put her away (in the end she pre-deceased him).[25] In reflecting upon and accounting for his response of hatred without any action issuing from it, the lawgiver may well have concluded that Jacob's judgment in the matter was that to do anything by way of reciprocating Laban's deception was unwise.[26] In a word, he was trapped. In turn, the Deuteronomist, with his concern for the woman, creates a law that ensures that once a man consummates a union he had better not resort to any trickery to undo it. For, should he do so, he will find himself even more locked into the marriage.

The second part of the law follows naturally from the first in that it considers the case where the man's allegation against his wife is justified, and she is convicted of harlotry in her father's house before her marriage. That the law is so 'naturally' constructed, however, is attributable to two factors. Deuteronomic draftmanship commonly pursues contrasting cases.[27] The second, more specific factor is the lawgiver's exploration of the story about Leah's daughter, Dinah. The first part of the law produces a case that is prompted by reflection, not directly to do with Dinah's situation, but nonetheless aided by Simeon and Levi's question about treating a daughter of Israel as a harlot. That is, consideration is given first to the offence done to the woman. Both the Dinah narrative and the law have this feature in common. The second part of the law is prompted by the Deuteronomist's closer scrutiny of Dinah's case.

As already noted, her status after her seduction provides the lawgiver with the hypothetical case of a woman in this position who marries someone other than her seducer. This case is made all the easier to construct because of the process of treating the ancient tradition as if it concerned matters strictly national; which means that the Deuteronomist ignores (because it was rejected) Shechem's request to marry Dinah after he had seduced her. In regard to

Dinah it would be natural to consider the issue that if she had married someone else she, or rather her parents, would not have been able to furnish a wedding night garment as a token of her virtue. Moreover, if her past is looked into carefully it is difficult to say whether she was forced by Shechem or whether she was biddable. There is some indication that she was willing. She took it upon herself to go out and visit the women of the area, and when Shechem encountered her, he, a prince, treated her with great tenderness. In the Deuteronomic law the question of the woman's harlotry is more starkly posed and is reckoned so heinous as to call for her execution. The harshness of this penalty, it may be noted, chimes with the severity of the punishment meted out to Shechem.

Punishments in antiquity are often well thought out. In the case of Shechem his offence is that as an uncircumcised Hivite he had seduced a daughter of Israel. His punishment was worked out by having him circumcised and using the occasion of his recovery from the operation to put him to the sword.[28] In the law the woman is put to death at her fasher's house because that is the place where she is assumed to have given up her virginity. This connection between the place of her misdeed and the place of her punishment may also be pertinent to the question of why it is the woman's parents, and not the husband and wife, who are supposed to have her wedding night cloth in their possession. It is unlikely that the consummation took place at her parents' home.[29] The fact that they possess it will reflect the Deuteronomic concern to make an Israelite responsible for keeping his house free from any taint of harlotry. The law that precedes in Deut 22:12 requires that an Israelite wear tassels on the corners of his garment for this very purpose. When the properly stained wedding garment is handed over to an Israelite head of household it constitutes proof that in the case of this particular daughter no harlotry has taken place in his house.

When Simeon and Levi aver that Shechem had made Dinah into a harlot, their judgment expressed their very high sexual standard and possibly also their anxiety about her status. We have seen how the Deuteronomist has drawn out this latter problem, specifically in regard to an Israelite's marrying a woman who may not be a virgin. This particular concern, however, is only one aspect of the problem posed for the Deuteronomist's reflection by the consequences of Shechem's unrestrained passion. As already indicated, the whole question of wrongful sexual relations is brought up, and the remaining sex laws in Deuteronomy 22 are attributable to the lawgiver's attempt to handle different possibilities that are suggested to him by the narrative in Genesis 34 with, in addition, the aid of the narrative about Sarah in Genesis 20.

The way in which these laws have been arrived at shows a very interesting method of using national traditions. The lawgiver, probably in a teaching capacity, has taken up the question about Dinah's harlotry raised in the last words of the narrative in Genesis 34 and asked his hearers: 'What is a comparable situation today, within Israel, in which an Israelite sister might be treated as a harlot?' The law in Deut 22:13–19 is one answer. Moreover, it proceeds (vss. 20, 21) to put forward, because of reflection upon the dubious nature of Dinah's role in the circumstances described in Genesis 34, the clear-cut case in which an Israelite girl is indeed guilty of harlotry.

In that this two-part law raises the issue of harlotry in the context of marriage, it is not surprising that the next law to be presented concerns the seduction of a married woman. This law on adultery is in Deut 22:22: 'If a man is found lying with the wife of another man, both of them shall die, the man who lay with the woman, and the woman; so thou shalt purge the evil from Israel.' But the construction of this law is largely attributable to the powerful influence of another, and in many respects closely related, Genesis tradition which vividly raises the topic of adultery, especially the question of the woman's guilt.

Sarah (in Genesis 20), like Dinah an ancestress of the Israelite nation, became sexually involved with a foreign prince on his territory. She was a married woman and yet she had let the king of Gerar think that she was Abraham's sister. It was only in a dream by night that the foreign monarch was warned that the woman was in fact a man's wife. Later reflection on the narrative must have raised (what the narrative itself does not) a pointed question about Sarah's role and responsibility in the entire matter. It is precisely this kind of reflection and narrowing of focus on some aspect of a narrative tradition that accounts for so many Deuteronomic laws.

In Genesis 20 a sentence of death is held over Abimelech should he have intercourse with Sarah, but no penalty is mentioned for her. As it happens, intercourse does not take place, but that is even more cause to formulate a law on the subject, to determine what the penalties should be if it does take place. The Deuteronomic law on adultery contains the judgment: 'Even both of them [gam-šᵉ*nehem*] shall die, the man who lay with the woman and the woman.' Taken in the context of legal history, the statement suggests that the reason for this adultery law is the desire to introduce a reform whereby the legal authorities wish to have jurisdiction over the woman's part in the offence as well as over the man's. Previously, so one would argue, the law punished the man but looked away from her, and left her fate in the hands of her husband.[30] More likely, however, given the framework in which the Deuteronomist constructs laws, the statement is directly related to the uncertainty that arises with Sarah about whether or not *in a situation within Israel* in which intercourse takes place a woman also deserves a penalty of death. In answering affirmatively the Deuteronomist is being consistent with his decision in the preceding law to execute the woman who had resorted to harlotry before her marriage. A linguistic connection between the law and the tradition makes the link in substance a virtual certainty. The expression 'a man's wife' (*bᵉᶜulat baᶜal*) is only found in biblical literature in these two places.

One final point about the use of the Sarah story is worth noting. From Abimelech's side of things Sarah came to him as previously unmarried, as Abraham's sister. If he had proceeded to consummate the marriage (as the Pharaoh in Genesis 12 had done) he would have found out that Sarah was not virginal. Reflection on this situation would have reinforced concern about Dinah's, and hence consideration of the case of the non-virginal bride in the law preceding the adultery law. We have noted before how the lawgiver ranges over more than one tradition if their situations are in some way similar.

The seduction of a betrothed woman is the next topic of concern in Deut 22:23–7. Again it can be argued that a consideration of the Shechem narrative has occasioned the formulation of the two-part law on the subject. At the point before Simeon and Levi intervened, Dinah's situation was being discussed in terms of betrothal. The ordinary way in which a woman becomes betrothed is for the man to make arrangements with her father. Seduction is an extraordinary way in which betrothal proceedings are likely to develop. After Shechem seduced Dinah his father entered into negotiations with Jacob in order to work out a bride-price. The lawgiver notes that the matter did not go beyond this stage, but would have done so if Shechem had been acceptable to Simeon and Levi.

With his consistent interest in first things,[31] the Deuteronomist has before him the suggestion of the first betrothed Israelite woman (the daughter of the original Israel), and he is led to consider wrongful sexual behaviour because of a woman's betrothed status. He is not taking this problem up directly from the Shechem tradition. It is nonetheless noteworthy that her status before her excursion into the midst of an alien cultural group is not in fact stated. That negotiations took place about a possible betrothal to Shechem probably do but need not imply that she was previously unattached. The discussions on the part of her family about her future were bogus. The lack of any explicit statement about Dinah's status would have provided additional scope for the Deuteronomist to raise the issue of the seduction of a betrothed woman. In other words, his procedure would be to have his audience consider both the possibility that she was unbetrothed and the possibility that she was already betrothed. His inclination to produce hypothetical cases must be kept in mind. Doubtless too, the seduction of a betrothed woman is considered because it is the case that falls between Dinah's apparent case, the seduction of an unbetrothed woman, and Sarah's case, which on one reading of the situation can be taken as presenting the problem of the seduction of a married woman. It is typical of this lawgiver to take up matters that are glossed over in a tradition and that require clarification for his audience. Deut 22:23–7 deals then with a betrothed woman who is seduced by an Israelite within an Israelite city, and one who is seduced, or forced, by an Israelite outside the bounds of a city. In the latter case she is not regarded as culpable because she may have cried for help, but no one responded.

An additional observation also helps to reveal the link between this two-part law and the Shechem tradition. The second part of it is most important because of the introduction of the law about the girl who cannot produce proof of her virginity. And the latter law, we have seen, stems from the Deuteronomist's reflection upon the Shechem story. The reason for considering the seduction of a betrothed woman in the open country, where there are no witnesses to the offence, is because the girl, if she does not report the matter, might be accused of harlotry by her spouse at the time they consummate their marriage. This point becomes clearer by noting that the seduction of a married woman in similarly unwitnessed circumstances is not considered. The reason is that the married woman cannot produce evidence of any offence because of her previous non-virginal state.

The dependence of the guilt or innocence of the betrothed

woman upon a geographical criterion, while doubtless a feature of proverbial legal lore,[32] is an issue that would be readily brought to mind by the Deuteronomist's review of Dinah's situation. She was seduced in a place beyond the boundary of her group: 'Now Dinah went out to visit the women of the land.'[33] It is a noticeable feature of the narrative that Dinah's guilt or innocence is left undetermined. Such indeterminacy would not have escaped the lawgiver and must be considered a factor in prompting him to decide upon the responsibility of a betrothed woman for her seduction.

Eventually the Deuteronomist turns his attention to the initial position of Dinah in the narrative, her seduction by Shechem, but again he switches his consideration to a situation that might arise within Israel. As previously observed, Dinah was probably an unbetrothed virgin when Shechem seduced her. After the seduction he sought to pay a bride-price to her father, whatever was asked, in the hope that she would become his wife. The matter was in a deliberately deceptive way both agreed to and denied because of Simeon and Levi's hostile intentions to Shechem. The Deuteronomist clarifies what he thinks the position should be for a comparable situation within Israel. The seducer must pay the father of the woman a fixed sum as bride-price, she must become his wife, because he has humbled her – the same expression as in Gen 34:2 – and he is denied the right to divorce her. The negotiations that took place in the Shechem story presuppose, in the natural way of things, that Jacob might refuse to give his deflowered daughter to Shechem. (As events turned out, with Jacob not involved, Shechem was denied Dinah.) Moreover, in the negotiations the bride-price offered by Shechem to Jacob was open to adjustment, with Jacob in the favourable bargaining position. The Deuteronomist rules out in his law for the Israelites any refusal on the part of the father, and fixes the bride-price at fifty shekels.

Dinah's case therefore furnished him with the issues in response to which he produces a definitive statement about what should be required in Israelite practice. It is, moreover, his critical reflection upon her case that accounts for the differences between his law and the earlier law on the subject in the *Mishpatim*. The latter allows for a variable bride-price from a seducer, and permits a father to refuse to give his daughter to him. The father's refusal might be motivated by economic reasons. According to the law in Ex 22:15, 16 (16, 17) a seducer must pay a sum whether or not the woman becomes his wife. The father, by refusing a marriage, collects the sum from the seducer and is in a position to arrange, for a price, another marriage. The Deuteronomist feels compelled to prevent such a manoeuvre. Like Simeon and Levi, he would note that the woman had been treated like a harlot, and in accord with his law in verses 13–19 he believes that an Israelite must not treat a woman in this way, but must marry her and permanently maintain her as his wife. Otherwise, if the woman marries someone else, she might find herself charged with not being a virgin and liable to face a death penalty for having committed harlotry.

The common factor about the denial of divorce and the permanent responsibility to maintain the woman as a wife in the two laws in Deut 22:13–19 and 22:28, 29 is too specific a correspondence to be explained solely on the grounds that the same lawgiver issues both of them. The fuller explanation is that each issues from reflection upon a common source – Genesis 34 (with the aid of Genesis 29).

The determining attitude that has shaped the Deuteronomic law on the seduction of an unbetrothed virgin is that the woman has been treated like a harlot. It is the same attitude, we have noted, that had been taken by Simeon and Levi in regard to Shechem's seduction of the apparently unbetrothed Dinah. The remedy provided by the law for the dishonoured woman is not that adopted by Simeon and Levi, but the reason for the difference is that Shechem was a Hivite or Canaanite. This same reason explains why the cryptic law against an ox and an ass ploughing together is found in the Deuteronomic code. Its inclusion at a point in Deuteronomy 22 preceding the sex laws was necessary to prepare the way for using the Genesis narrative for national purposes.[34] The Israelite group consciousness revealed by Simeon and Levi in the narrative becomes all pervasive in the Deuteronomic treatment of it. The story is purged of its foreign elements and used to suggest hypothetical matters pertinent to the national scene. Hence the sex laws, while certainly deriving from the Deuteronomist's critical attention to the story, do not apply to Shechem's case.

The cryptic aspect of the ox and ass law is not without interest. It is perhaps mainly attributable to the Genesis material where the potential for a cryptic construction already exists because of the name Hamor (Ass) and the related use of the ox in reference to Israel. Another factor, however, may be pertinent. The ox and ass law can be perceived as critical of the original Israel's opposition to, from the Deuteronomic viewpoint, the morally correct action of Simeon and Levi in responding to their sister's dishonoured status. In Deut 33:8–11 the Deuteronomist's high regard for Levi stands out impressively in contrast to Jacob's condemnation of him (and Simeon) in Gen 49:5–7. To criticise the eponymous head of one's nation is, however, a risky and sensitive undertaking. One has to presume that such criticism could provoke a hostile reaction among some circles in the Deuteronomist's time. Hence the resort to subtle, allusive, and perhaps even jesting language so that the full brunt of the criticism is lightened.[35]

The name of Israel's daughter, Dinah, means 'judgment' and must be seen as significant in light of the Deuteronomist's legal preoccupation with the Shechem material. The name can be taken to mean the case of Israel's daughter that requires judgment, or even legal review. This observation presupposes that the name is artificial. In support of this presupposition attention can be drawn to the other names in the narrative. Hamor and Shechem, which mean 'ass' and 'the shoulder of an ass', cannot be the original Canaanite names of this man and his son. Rather they are derogatory, artificial Hebrew constructions.

Bilhah

Both in its present form in Genesis and in its impact on the Deuteronomist, the Shechem story had become didactically oriented. Its focus had narrowed to the subject of harlotry and Israel's daughter(s). Like many a piece of wisdom counsel on the subject from the book of Proverbs, its underlying intention was to warn young men to avoid the example of Shechem's passion. In this regard it is noteworthy that the narrative that follows the Shechem story contains a notice about how Reuben, Israel's son,[1] lay with his father's concubine, Bilhah. Likewise, the law that follows the ones in Deuteronomy 22, which are prompted by the Shechem narrative, concerns a man, an Israelite, who offends by having intercourse with his father's wife.[2] The Deuteronomic code of laws,[3] unlike the lists of laws in Leviticus 18 and Leviticus 20, contains only this one prohibition relating to forbidden degrees of affinity. The influence of the Genesis tradition on the Deuteronomist helps to explain this limitation.

The position in Genesis 35 of the notice about Reuben's loose conduct with Bilhah appears to be arbitrary. Probably, however, its placement at a point following the Shechem narrative is due to the didactic orientation introduced into the final arrangement of the Genesis material. A characteristic of most hortatory material, the book of Proverbs and the Deuteronomic instruction, for example, is a fondness for associating like with like, or presenting contrasting cases. Either Reuben's action has been compared to Shechem's with the additional thought that one is an Israelite and the other is not, or, the topic of harlotry as it related to Dinah, a daughter of Israel, is complemented by a similar topic being raised in the case of a son of Israel.

The law contains the curiously figurative language that a man should not uncover his father's skirt. This way of referring to intercourse with a woman seems insulting to her and would be contrary to the Deuteronomist's usual sensitivity to a woman's honour.[4] The intention is otherwise, however. The skirt (*kanap*) as symbolic of a wife requires explanation. The best clue is to be found in such texts as Ruth 3:9 and Ezek 16:8. In the former Ruth asks Boaz to spread his skirt over her as a token that he will marry her. In the latter God is thought of as taking Jerusalem to wife, again by spreading his skirt over her and covering her nakedness. The meaning surely is that the male's removal of his garment and placing it upon the woman is for the symbolic purpose that he will obtain a new use for it. She now becomes his skirt, to be put on by him, that is, as a wife. Precise confirmation for this symbolic meaning will be forth-coming when we interpret the sandal and foot symbolism in the Ruth story.[5]

Two laws to do with clothing come between the prohibition against ploughing with an ox and an ass and the law about the man who, when he takes a wife, claims that she is not a virgin. The first prohibits the wearing of wool and linen together. I have argued elsewhere that the reason for the prohibition is the association of wool with purity and linen with harlotry.[6] Worn together they con-stitute a clash of opposites and hence, consistent with the other laws in this part of the code, an example of an unnatural or undesir-able mixture. The subject of harlotry is a particularly appropriate one at this point in the code because of the dominant influence of the Genesis tradition about Shechem's treatment of Dinah.

The second law about clothing consists of a positive injunction to Israelites that they place tassels on the corners (*kan^{e}pot*) of their garments. The similar law in Num 15:37–9 states the reason for the law. The Israelites are to look upon these tassels with a view to avoiding loose, wanton behaviour. They are not to let impure thoughts (the verb 'to commit fornication' is used) or lustful eyes overcome them. Again it is significant that this law is presented between the ox and ass law, which was concerned with Shechem's desire for Dinah, and just before the law about harlotry and an Israelite woman. In light of both the symbolism about a man's new wife as his garment and the position of the tassels law a more specific interpretation of the latter presents itself. The law's bias is toward the subject of marriage. The garment in question, upon which the tassels are to be placed, derives its significance from a man's taking a wife, the occasion of his spreading his skirt over her and her becoming his 'skirt' or 'garment'. Upon that woman, and that woman alone, may he look with desire. The tasselled garment around his body serves as a constant reminder of his attachment to his wife.[7] That is why the law is a positive command and not a prohibition.

In the law that follows the tassels law a man takes a woman as a wife, has intercourse with her, and then detaches himself from her and makes it known that she had not been a virgin when he took her. His allegations are proved false by the production of the stained wedding-night garment. It is this cloth that constitutes proof of her purity, and contrariwise, the lack of it, proof of harlotry on her part. We are reminded of the preceding prohibition against wearing wool (a symbol of purity) and linen (a symbol of harlotry) together. One consequence of the production of the wedding-night garment in clearing the woman's reputation is that the husband must maintain her as his wife throughout his life-time. Again it is interesting that a garment becomes associated with the permanent attachment of a man to his wife, just as in the tassels law the garment is supposed to serve a similar function.

When the law prohibiting a son from taking his father's wife goes on to state in an ambiguously synonymous fashion, 'Nor shall he uncover his father's skirt', the reason for so stating it is noteworthy. The literal meaning of the words is the opposite of the figurative. Moreover, the literal meaning is a shocking one. It refers to a son's direct sexual interference with his father. This use of opposite meanings,[8] in which the literal is more shocking than the intended figurative one, is a deliberate attempt to arouse disgust in the recipients of the law. One factor in their use in this particular law may have to do with counteracting a prevailing casual attitude among the law's recipients in regard to their ancestor's seduction of Bilhah. A similar tendency underlies the ox and ass law, only in that instance the intention was to direct attention to, for the purpose of opposing, Jacob's complacency about Shechem's seduction of Dinah.

While the law about the father's skirt does not in fact treat the woman in a light, contemptible way (indeed indirectly its intention is the opposite), the underlying focus of attention has been Reuben, Israel's eldest son. Dinah played this role in the preceding laws because she was Israel's one and only daughter. Reuben has already figured in the law of the first-born because of his status and because he was the son of Israel's unloved wife, Leah. Understandably, Reuben's seduction of his father's concubine must have occasioned much anguish among those who preserved their group's traditions. On the one hand is this offence while on the other is his special, almost sacrosanct position as his father's first-born. To enjoy this privilege was to anticipate a larger share of any inherit-

ance and to be fondly and fancifully spoken of by a father as the
'first-fruits of my strength' and 'my might'. Jacob so refers to him
in Gen 49:3 and the Deuteronomic law of the first-born repeats
the former phrase in support of awarding a double share of the
inheritance to the eldest son. Jacob also, however, in his final words
to Reuben in Genesis 49, recounts his sexual offence and hence in
Genesis there already exists an anguished assessment of him. The
picture is much the same in Deuteronomy. The law of the first-
born continues to underline the significance of being a man's first-
fruits, and elsewhere in Deuteronomy great importance is attached
to the bearing of children and their social function in enhancing a
man's reputation. The law of the father's skirt clearly indicates,
however, a shocked reaction to Reuben's conduct with Bilhah. In
Moses' last words to the sons of Israel – a form of address modelled
on Jacob's valediction in Genesis 49 – the Deuteronomist betrays
his barely positive affirmation of Reuben: 'Let Reuben live and not
die; yet let his men be few.'⁹ These words may convey the view
that the effect of Reuben's specially endowed powers of generation
was muted by the manner in which he exercised them. They would
constitute another superb example of the proverbial view that a
man and his deeds meet with exact retribution: an abundance of
progenital strength, if misused, results in the deprivation of offspring.

If the law of the father's skirt stands in condemnation of Reuben,
the following law prohibiting a eunuch from entering Israel's
assembly of the Lord switches its attention to the other, positive
facet of Reuben's existence – his pre-eminent powers of generation
because he represents the first-fruits of Jacob-Israel's strength. A
eunuch represents the complete negation of the Deuteronomist's
firmly fixed and ideologically rich belief in the value and significance
of progeny. When Jacob in prescient mood before his death
assembles his sons the nature of this assembly centres on the notion
of the continuing communal existence and fortune of Israel as a
tribal unity. The potential for perpetuating its existence by progeny
is basic to such a conception. Little wonder then that many of the
pronouncements assess this aspect of a family and that the very first
saying is about Reuben, how he is Jacob's first-born and how he
possesses progenital strength to an extraordinary degree. A similar
evaluation of the nation Israel lies at the core of the Deuteronomist's thinking. The entire setting of his work is shaped along
the lines suggested by Jacob's assembly in Genesis 49. Hence

Moses, also in a seer's role at the end of his life, gathers together the tribes of Israel and lays out what is required for their future. The moral tone of his assessment is sharper, more elevated, and the assessment itself is more wide-ranging than the original Israel's. One result is that the latter's assembly now enjoys the idealised name of the assembly of the Lord. In excluding a eunuch from entrance into this assembly the Deuteronomist, working out of the above background, feels that a eunuch's deficiency is irreconcilable with the group's existence and purpose.

Both Shechem in Genesis 34 and Reuben in Genesis 35 commit the one offence that causes wise men, those in the book of Proverbs, for example, to go on at great length about the folly of being caught up in sexual desire. Being wise, however, they would also be capable of considering the opposite state of affairs, namely, a man given to no passion whatsoever. They would declare this to be folly also. A characteristic of this lawgiver that is derived from his wisdom background is his fondness for presenting contrasting cases.[10] This factor is also observable in the presentation of his law prohibiting a eunuch entrance into Israel's assembly.

THE DAUGHTERS OF LOT

In the same measure as the sages in Proverbs cover the ground in
dealing with the topic of sexual licence, so too the Deuteronomist –
with the interesting difference that he covers the examples of such
licence in the book of Genesis. From the inter-family case of
Israel's first-born son's seduction of his father's concubine, he
proceeds to the even more dramatic case of the double seduction of
a bibulous father, Lot, by his first-born daughter followed by his
second-born.[1] Bastard children came of this union: the ancestors
of the Moabites and the Ammonites. Hence the Deuteronomist,
after his law that prohibits a man from taking his father's wife and
one that prohibits a eunuch entrance into Israel's assembly, sets
down the law: 'No bastard shall enter the assembly of the Lord;
even to the tenth generation none of his descendants shall enter the
assembly of the Lord.'[2]

Confirmation that Lot's case inspired such a prohibition in
regard to children born of an incestuous union is to be noted by the
fact that the very next law also excludes for all time ('even to the
tenth generation') the Ammonites and the Moabites from Israel's
assembly.[3] The reasons for their exclusion are given in terms of
their harsh treatment of the Israelites at the time of the exodus.
Moses, so we are to understand, is making these laws and is speaking out of his own experience with these two groups. We can infer
the interesting belief that the quality of a later generation is judged
by that of the first. The Ammonites and Moabites had nothing
going for them from the very beginning; no wonder that they
behaved badly at the exodus and one can expect nothing from them
in the future.[4] Wisdom belief underlies such thinking.[5]

The primary motivation for the Deuteronomic law is probably
the ambivalence that might exist, and which the Deuteronomist
does not wish to exist, of whether or not Lot's daughters were
justified in their action. The Deuteronomist places much positive
emphasis on fecundity. Lot's daughters had no other means to
perpetuate their family line and hence their decision to obtain offspring by their father. Indeed, the problem as presented in Genesis

is even more pressing. If they do not act there will be no way at all to preserve offspring on the earth. The Genesis tradition could be understood as sympathetic.

Again, then, a problem in an ancient tradition is posed. The resolution of it from the Deuteronomist's point of view is clear. He is not in the least impressed. For him it is a case of incest comparable to Reuben's. Only he concentrates on the specific result of the act, the birth of bastards, that is, children born of an incestuous union. The reason is partly his interest in the Ammonites and the Moabites, partly, that unlike Reuben's union, this one did result in offspring, but mainly his shocked reaction to the sexual activity in question.

The Genesis tradition regarding Lot's drunkenness and seduction is placed just after the sequence of material about the destruction of Sodom and Gomorrah. Certain observations can be made which suggest that the episode may stand in a closer relationship to the preceding material than has been hitherto noted. There can be little doubt that already in the tradition Lot is viewed in a critical light. Speiser underlines this aspect of the narrative although he is curiously positive about the sexual activity of Lot and his two daughters.[6] For Lot to let himself become drunk would surely be viewed in a mocking light. In going over his material for the purpose of arranging it, the compiler of these Genesis traditions would appear to have been uncomfortable with Lot's response to the homosexual request of his fellow inhabitants of Sodom. Lot had attempted to ward off their desires for his male guests by offering instead his two virgin daughters. Reflecting on this offer, the compiler would probably have little or no feeling for the exigencies of the situation and for the fact that emotional responses are often inevitably non-reflective in character. His conclusion would be that a man who treats his daughters as harlots to be abused by other men might find that his action will meet with a mirroring response: they in turn will abuse him sexually. Given the consistent pattern in the Genesis material of deeds meeting with exact retribution, this interpretation of Lot's seduction would fit into it. The episode would therefore stand as a sequel to the preceding material about him.

Two further observations underline the link between the two episodes.[7] In each an outrageous act takes place because it is understood that priority has to be given to another need. Lot offers his two daughters for the sexual gratification of the inhabitants of

Sodom, and he does so because the duty of hospitality to guests requires that he protects them, in this instance, from the homosexual lusts of these inhabitants. Lot's daughters, in turn, engage in incestuous acts because, it is implied, the need to perpetuate the family line, which will also serve to save the human species, takes precedence.

The second link between the two incidents is a contrasting one. Ordinarily, men of the depraved mob mentality of Sodom can be expected to respond with alacrity to the offer of two women. These men, however, are different in that they only respond sexually to men. When we turn to the initiative of Lot's daughters in seducing their father we observe that their desire was the natural one of seeking sexual relations with other men, but their situation was such that they ended up having unnatural union with their father, a deed that ordinarily would be wholly repugnant. The homosexual lust of the Sodomites led to Lot's decision to exploit his daughters, who are passive in this situation. The affliction of blindness, however, prevents the Sodomites from gratifying their homosexuality. Their lust being rendered inactive is, in a way, made to fit the girl's passivity. By contrast, Lot's daughters initiate the action with their father. Moreover, they complete it because having made him drunk he becomes an instrument to be used by them. Drunkenness and blindness are often viewed as interrelated.[8] Here there is a link between one and the other in that it is blindness that prevents unnatural sexual activity taking place in one situation and drunkenness that enables it to happen in the other.

TAMAR

In Genesis 37 the long story about Joseph begins but is surprisingly
interrupted in Genesis 38 by what appears to be a quite haphazard
insertion of an account of Judah's family problems.[1] In fact, the
sequence is far from haphazard. What has occurred is that the
initial chapter of the Joseph story relates the events of his youth in
such a way that they point forward proleptically to events that
involve the destiny of the entire family of Jacob, including Judah.
To ascribe to a man's youth such anticipatory significance is not
solely a powerful story-telling device but reveals strong wisdom
overtones – a feature not unexpected in the light of the well-
recognised wisdom character of the entire Joseph story. Instruction
in wisdom is usually directed at young men and a major aim is to
convince them that the acquisition of it in their youth will determine their future. The many proverbs designed to train them in the
way that they should walk presuppose such a view. A youth, such
as Joseph, specially endowed with the blessings of wisdom can be
guaranteed to have an unusually rich and influential future.

Once this feature of the initial account of Joseph's life is understood, the insertion of the Judah story becomes intelligible. The
event that determines his destiny is the dramatic one involving the
sale of Joseph to Egypt. In typical wisdom fashion one man, Judah,
is held individually responsible for Joseph's humiliation.[2] It is he
who in his craftiness does not see the point of leaving Joseph to die
in the pit into which he has been cast. Instead he sees profit to be
gained from the situation. His suggestion that Joseph be sold to
traders is agreed to by the other brothers present at the scene.
Judah's initiative in the whole affair brands him as culpable for the
sale of his brother and, further, for the grief that he brings upon his
father. Thus Jacob is deceived into thinking that his son is dead
and gone. The deception is achieved by the clever and simple ruse
of killing an animal, dipping Joseph's coat in its blood, and having
Jacob acknowledge that a wild beast has devoured him.[3]

The Joseph story is discontinued at the end of Genesis 37 and the
narrative of Judah and his family introduced. The specific reason

for its introduction at this point is that the inexorable law of retribution, which is such a characteristic feature of the fitting together of so much of the Genesis material, is being applied to Judah. He is about to experience what it is like to lose a son. The retribution is possibly even more exact. Jacob had known of the intense antagonism of all his sons to his favourite, Joseph. In a sense, when Joseph 'died' he was bereft of all his sons. In other words, their antagonism to him had removed their father's affection for them and it is little wonder that when mourning Joseph he could not be comforted by them. Judah, in turn, finds himself not just perplexed by the loss of one son but by the dismal prospect of the loss of all three.

An element of retribution may also have been seen in the fact that, just as Joseph, largely on Judah's instigation, was forcibly removed from his family by being taken to Egypt, so Judah 'went down from his brothers', and became involved in a Canaanite marriage and, by implication, Canaanite ways.[4] In Genesis 49, when Jacob looks back on Judah's actions and evaluates them, much is made – negatively – of his Canaanite connection. Judah had three sons born to him in this new place of residence, and for his first-born, Er, he arranged a marriage to Tamar. Er died because of something displeasing to the deity. Onan was then obliged to take Tamar and by making her pregnant was supposed to continue the line of his dead brother – hence the father's also. Onan was un-willing to fulfil this levirate duty – doubtless his motivation would be an economic one[5] – and in the process of intercourse with Tamar he spilled his seed on the ground. He too displeased the deity and was stricken from existence. The duty of continuing the family line then fell upon Shelah, but he was not of age, and in any case, Judah had had to take note that the loss of his sons and the extinction of his line were the fearful consequence of the association with Tamar.

We in fact hear nothing more about the third son, Shelah. Attention becomes focused on Tamar and the rest of the story describes her daring and courageous action for the purpose of acquiring a child to continue the line of the family into which she had married. Disguising herself as a harlot, she encounters Judah at a place called Enaim and there becomes pregnant by him. He has not recognised her and he pledges to give a kid from his flock for her services. She requests that by way of making good his pledge he leave her his seal-and-cord and his staff. The story proceeds to its dramatic conclusion. Judah learns that his daughter-in-law is pregnant by harlotry, he pronounces a death sentence upon her, but she reveals his identifying symbols that mark him as the father of her expected offspring. He then acknowledges her right to obtain a child from within his family. Moreover, his own grim dilemma of being without offspring after the generation of Shelah is solved in an almost tragi-comic way: his blind passion for the harlot at Enaim has made him the father of twins. If the theme of event and mirroring counter-event plays a large role in the writing up of the Judah story, then it may be noted that the precarious position of Judah in regard to his future existence as the head of a line possibly reflects the precarious state of Joseph, in that he had in fact not died but continued to live on in Egypt. In trying to eliminate Joseph's claim to his father's favour, with a view to obtaining it himself, Judah brings upon himself a fate similar to Joseph's. Interestingly, Joseph's own line was perpetuated by the birth of twins and equally interesting, in each case, the first-born was usurped by the second-born. Such parallels suggest a special rivalry between these two brothers in the broader context of establishing dominance for the purpose of acquiring the blessings of Jacob's name.

The correctness of the preceding explanation of why the story of Judah interrupts the development of the Joseph story is confirmed by the allusions to both stories in the saying about Judah in Gen 49:8–12. Just as elements of the Joseph story in Genesis 37 pointed forward to significant events in his life and the lives of Judah and his brothers, so the characteristic feature of the sayings of Jacob in Genesis 49 is that they look back on significant events in the lives of his sons, Judah included. The aura of wisdom that surrounds the youthful Joseph is matched by the prescience of the aged and dying Jacob. It is he who surrounded by his sons – like a wise master waited upon by his disciples – summarises the to and fro of their ways. The first saying about Reuben, and the next about Simeon and Levi, incorporate references tot he significant events in their lives: Reuben's seduction of his father's concubine, and Simeon and Levi's action against Hamor and his group.

The sayings are elegant, and a great deal of thought has gone into their composition. Their most common poetical features are plays upon words (e.g. Gen 49:8, 16) and the use of animal imagery (Israel is an ox, Judah is a lion, Er and Onan are asses, likewise Issachar; Dan is a serpent, Naphtali is a hind, Benjamin is a wolf). They attempt to be proverbial in that they encapsulate in an allusive way the outstanding biographical facts and the essential

nature of the person in question. With these sophisticated features
in mind, the interpretation of the highly allusive Judah saying
becomes relatively straightforward. One exaggerates a little by
stating that no text in the bible has received so much attention as
that concerning Judah, and no traditional interpretation has been
so wide of the mark as the usual Messianic explanation that is
attributed to it.

Certain features from Genesis 37 and 38 have been incorporated
in 49:8-12 to convey Jacob's assessment of his son, Judah. The
events of Joseph's early youth had impinged upon Judah's life and
these are seen to constitute a salient aspect of his fortunes. Joseph
had his two dreams in each of which his brothers, first as sheaves
of the field and then as stars of the sky, bowed down to him. Whatever reality these dreams were to anticipate, it was preceded by
that of the brothers' antagonism in which Judah had a forceful role.
They rid themselves of the dreamer and in doing so Judah's
brothers 'heeded him'.[6] In Gen 49:8-12, after other events have
intervened and Joseph has attained the position that his dreams
foretold, Jacob with the objectivity of ironic detachment looks back
on the early situation of Judah's vanquishing of Joseph. 'Judah,
thou', Jacob emphasises,[7] 'thy brothers were praising. Thy hand
was on the neck of thine enemies. Thy father's sons were bowing
down before thee.' The reference is surely to Judah's usurping the
position that Joseph's dreams had outlined for himself. The
'enemies' will be none other than Jacob and Joseph. Such enmity
was already indicated in that Joseph had brought a bad report of
his brothers to his father.[8] Jacob had favoured Joseph – with love
and a special coat. In hating him,[9] the brothers were also being
hostile to their father. That the latter's sons were bowing down
before Judah means that Jacob the father was excluded; so too was
Joseph because he was the one who should have been receiving the
homage. Jacob had already accused Simeon and Levi (in the preceding saying in Gen 49:5-7) of enmity against himself: in slaying
the man, Hamor, they had at the same time hamstrung – as one
does an enemies' animals – the ox, Israel. In the case of Judah,
enmity within the clan or family is again in mind.

In his sons' treacherous treatment of Joseph, Judah is singled out
by Jacob in Gen 49:9 as the wild beast that allegedly tore Joseph to
pieces and left only a blood-stained part of his coat as evidence by
which Jacob had to acknowledge the disaster: 'A wild beast has
devoured him. Joseph is torn, torn [*ṭarop ṭorap*]'.[10] Jacob in Gen

49:9 alludes to this episode: 'A lion's whelp is Judah: from the prey of my son [*mitterep beni*] thou didst come up.' Judah had 'stooped and couched as a lion' and Jacob, addressing all his sons in this retrospective scene, asks who would arouse him – a possible reference to their acquiescence in the disposal of Joseph. The fact that Judah is compared to a young lion is possibly a sarcastic indication that he had, like a young lion in imitation of its mother, only gone through the motions of slaying Joseph.

The allusions in the saying up to this point are to details of the Joseph story in Genesis 37. From this point on they are to details of the Judah story in Genesis 38. Thus there is a complete change from the leonine imagery to imagery concerning lineal descent, which is precisely the subject-matter of the Judah narrative. The saying in fact focuses on the heart of the problem with which Judah finds himself confronted. One obvious purpose of having his son Er married to Tamar was to perpetuate the family line. When the consequence of this union was the death of Er, the levirate custom was invoked. This too proved unsuccessful, because of Onan's action of withdrawing from intercourse. With the latter's death the responsibility shifted to Shelah (*šlh*),[11] but Judah was reluctant to involve his one remaining son in a union with Tamar because of the fearful results that had flowed from the two previous unions. The saying is resonant with double meanings which despite their cleverness are in a down to earth way all about Judah's dilemma.

'The sceptre', Jacob comments, 'was not departing from Judah, nor the staff from between his legs until Shelah [*šlh*][12] would go in [to Tamar].' The sceptre or staff symbolises the headship of a line and also connotes generative power. The latter aspect is emphasised in that the staff between the feet or legs alludes to the male sexual organ.[13] Already in the Judah story a similar symbolism can be seen in the circumstances surrounding Judah's intercourse with the disguised Tamar. Judah promised a kid from his flock by way of paying for her services. He never managed to hand it over because he could not find her. Little did he know at the time that the woman would turn out to be the member of his family who bears him the offspring that would sustain his own line. The kid from his flock is possibly pointing in a figurative way to this development. When he promised the kid, Tamar had requested that he pledge payment of it by offering her his seal-and-cord and his staff. There may be a double meaning in this reference to the staff. She had just received his 'staff' and her aim was to achieve the continuation of his line, thus ensuring that his heraldic staff would be passed on to the next generation. However that may be, in the saying the reference to Judah's staff not passing on 'until Shelah goes in' is to Judah's dilemma in preventing Shelah from going into Tamar, because he fears that, like his brothers, his death would ensue. In holding him back, however, Judah is blocking the means of continuing his family line. The cryptic and abbreviated phrase 'until Shelah goes in' cleverly conveys the hesitancy and reluctance of Judah to let Shelah go into – Tamar.[14] The phrase that follows, 'And to him [that is, the child born if and when Shelah takes Tamar] would be the obedience of the peoples', expresses the desired glory that Jacob assumes Judah sought when he usurped his brother, Joseph. The words echo the great blessing that is associated with the birth of a child to a patriarch. In Gen 48:1–6 Jacob informs Joseph, who stands before him with his two offspring, that they will bear the blessing of future fruitfulness and the creation of a company of peoples.[15] In Jacob's words to Judah in Gen 49:8–12, he points out to him how he, Judah, would dearly wish to have Shelah stand before him with his offspring in order for him to pass on the blessing of a renowned line. Such a desirable outcome, however, had not worked out for Judah, and the fault lay in his wretched treatment of Joseph.

Having Joseph removed forcibly to foreign parts, where events were to take a better turn for him, Judah found himself voluntarily removing himself to Canaanite parts, where untoward events were to overtake him. From being the young lion that had marred Joseph, he became the father of asses that began to destroy themselves and, as a consequence, his own future line. Before turning to these allusions in the next part of the saying, some preliminary observations are necessary in order to comprehend the figurative language.

First, Canaanites are sometimes derisively compared to asses. Hamor, which is Hebrew for ass, was the head of the Canaanite group, the Hivites. Jacob's son, Issachar, is mockingly compared to an ass in Gen 49:14 because he reversed the relationship that should exist between the Canaanites and Israel. In Gen 9:25–7 Noah curses Canaan to become a slave of Shem, the ancestor of Israel. Issachar, the name means 'hired man', is said by Jacob to have become an ass who bowed his shoulder (Shechem in Hebrew and the name of Hamor's son in Genesis 34) to become a slave at forced labour. The comparison of him to an ass indicates that he has effectively transformed himself into a Canaanite, of whom servitude should be or is the leading characteristic. Judah married a Canaanite woman in Canaan and hence his sons are half-Canaanite. In Gen 49:11 we shall see that the reference to Judah's ass, *'ir*, is intended by Jacob to echo the name of Judah's son, Er (*'er*), and to bring out the fact of his Canaanite nature. Likewise, the parallel reference to the son of the she-ass (*b*e*ni-'*a*ton*) is intended to recall Judah's second son, Onan, by his Canaanite wife, whose name is (significantly perhaps) omitted in Genesis 38.

A second observation concerns the use of the vine imagery in the saying. The vine with its almost observable reproduction and luxurious growth is an appropriate plant to invoke by way of speaking figuratively about human increase. Throughout biblical literature it is employed in this fashion.[16] Its figurative use in the Judah saying is especially suitable because of the overriding concern with the problem of his progeny.

When Jacob describes Judah as, 'Binding his ass to the vine and the son of the she-ass to the choice vine', he alludes to the union of first Er and then Onan to Tamar. This union represents Judah's attempt to increase his stock. Although Tamar should not be identified with the vine, it is noteworthy that her own name refers to the palm-tree, and in the Song of Songs 7:8–10 (7–9) features of it and the vine become synonymous attributes of the breasts of the bride.[17] Tamar is the means by which Judah's vine is to sprout new branches. However, if one tethers asses to a vine, it is destroyed. Hence this figurative language, if taken in its literal aspect, brilliantly conveys the effect of Er and Onan's marriage to Tamar. The union with her led to their death and consequently to the withering away of Judah's vine.

Jacob continues, 'He [Judah] was washing his cloak in wine and his robe in the blood of grapes.' Such a strange action is only intelligible if we recall that Judah in disposing of Joseph washed his special coat in the blood of an animal in order to deceive Jacob into believing that his son was dead. Just as the reference to the *son* of the she-ass is a deliberate clue to a human meaning, so too is the reference to the *blood* of grapes. With terrible irony Jacob is describing to Judah the burden he had to bear because of his action against Joseph. The irony is that whereas Joseph's death was not real even though the real blood stains on his coat indicated that it was, Judah's two sons were truly dead; and the unreal gesture that Jacob attributes to Judah of washing his own clothes in the imaginary blood of grapes conveyed this dreadful reality. In imaginary terms their death corresponds to the scene of destruction that is conjured up by asses trampling and consuming and pressing out the juices of the grapes of the vine to which they are tied. The nadir of Judah's situation is thus described and the description corresponds to the elements of the narrative in Genesis 38.

The unexpected upturn in Judah's situation is brought about by Tamar's initiative in disguising herself as a harlot and waylaying Judah when he was on his way to a sheep-shearing festivity.[18] As a result of this encounter twins were born to him and his family line was saved from extinction. The last verse of the saying alludes to this unusual climax to Judah's problem. The first part is about his harlotry and the second about its results, the twins. Doubtless Jacob is pointing out in a mocking way that this lion of a man only achieved continuance of his name in the most precarious of ways, through harlotry. 'Dull were the eyes [*'enayim*] from wine, and white were the teeth from milk.' These words continue to reveal all the literary tricks of the previous part of the saying.[19] The word for eyes is intended to recall the place, Enaim (*'enayim*), where Judah met the harlot.[20] From wine in the figurative sense of blood, there is, as plain literary sense would require, a switch to its normal meaning. Together, the eyes dull from wine at Enaim, the references describe the typical combination of inebriation from wine and desire for a woman. In Prov 23:26–35 such a combination is spelled out, the rare word for dullness of the eyes (*ḥaklili*) is used, and the passage underlines the confusion of sight that arises from drinking. Such is implied in Judah's case in that he did not recognise his own daughter-in-law when having intercourse with her. The fact that she had veiled her face does not entirely mitigate his lack of recognition.[21]

If the word 'eyes' is playing a subtle role in recalling Judah's going into the harlot at Enaim, then the reference to the 'Teeth white from milk' points to the twins who were born of the union and who were weaned at her breasts to become the progenitors of Judah's line.[22] The word Enaim also means 'twin springs', in fact such is the meaning of the place-name, and this other meaning serves as a link between the two parts of the line. The reason is that the word in this sense figuratively conveys the notion of fertility. In the Song of Songs 4:12 the bride is compared to a sealed fountain (in Song of Songs 7:8[7] she is compared to a palm-tree, Tamar, and her breasts to its cluster of dates), and in Deut 33:28, in the parallel literary work to Genesis 49, the expression 'the fountain of Jacob' refers to his descendants. The dual form of the word for teeth also enables the author to suggest the meaning of twins. Confirmation for this correlation between a set of teeth and twins is to be seen in another context of love-making. In the Song of Songs 4:2 the bridegroom describes the teeth of his bride as 'like a flock of ewes just shorn which have come up fresh from the dipping; each ewe has twins and none has cast a lamb'. The teeth are compared to the regular pattern that is suggested by the sight of the fresh, white ewes each with a twin lamb on either side of it. But more than that there is an allusion to the bride's future fertility. The language constitutes a remarkable echo of the love-making between Judah and Tamar. He was on his way to his sheep-shearing when he lay with her, and he promised her a kid from his flock for her services. What came instead were the twin children who kept his family stock on the increase.

The Deuteronomist has a law on levirate marriage:

> If brothers dwell together, and one of them dies and has no son, the wife of the dead shall not be married outside the family to a stranger; her husband's brother shall go in to her, and take her as his wife, and perform the duty of a husband's brother to her. And the first son whom she bears shall succeed to the name of his brother who is dead, that his name may not be blotted out of Israel. And if the man does not wish to take his brother's wife, then his brother's wife shall go up to the gate to the elders, and say, 'My husband's brother refuses to perpetuate his brother's name in Israel; he will not perform the duty of a husband's brother to me.' Then the elders of his city shall call him, and speak to him: and if he persists, saying, 'I do not wish to take her,' then his brother's wife shall go up to him in the presence of the elders, and pull his sandal off his foot, and spit in his face; and she shall answer and say, 'So shall it be done to the man who does not build up his brother's house.' And its name shall be called in Israel, The house of him that had his sandal pulled off.[23]

It is commonly thought that the first part of this law is a general statement of the levirate custom, a description of the ordinary circumstances in which it is invoked.[24] We have seen, however, that such general statements of law are quite *un*characteristic of this lawgiver; rather the tendency is invariably in the direction of a limiting set of circumstances. This law is no different. Closer scrutiny reveals that it is prompted by a need to legislate for the particular circumstances in which the head of the family, the father, is dead.

The crucial observations for this correct view of the law have been made by David Daube.[25] A fundamental observation is that if the father, the *paterfamilias*, were alive there would be no need for the law because he would compel his son's compliance with the custom. The law's formulation makes this point all the clearer. If the father were alive we would not expect the law to state, as it does, the position in terms of brothers living together on the undivided paternal estate. We would expect consistent reference to his role in attending to the problem of lineage caused by the death of a childless married son. Instead of the statement about how the dead man's brother must marry the widow, we would expect a description of the father's order to his son, the *levir*, to take the widow and raise a child by her. When the law goes on to deal with a son's refusal to comply with the levirate custom, there is no mention of the father's exerting any pressure. That is remarkable – if he were still around. In face of the son's persistent refusal the authorities are to press compliance, but such disobedience would hardly arise, especially in light of the severe Deuteronomic law about the son who disobeys his parents,[26] if the father were alive.

The entire law is inspired by the Deuteronomist's reflection upon the Tamar tradition. The problem which stands out in regard to the fulfilment of the levirate custom in that story is Judah's failure to ensure that his third son, Shelah, goes into Tamar. But this problem is essentially the same one that arose because of the second son's refusal, *which was hidden from his father*, to do his duty by his dead brother's widow. Stripping the story of its idiosyncratic features, the Deuteronomist is presented with the problem that lies before us in his levirate law: what to do in the absence of the enforcing authority of a father when a son refuses to act on behalf of his dead brother. Another major motivating factor for the Deuteronomist's interest in the problem will have been his negative reaction to the fact that Tamar had to resort to harlotry in order to obtain a child, that she was forced to fulfil in a devious way the intent of the levirate custom. The lawgiver, objecting to such a degrading development involving a woman, pursues the element of disgrace and locates its true source in the attitude of the male. The result is that a woman is required by the law to heap obloquy upon a man.

From the Deuteronomic legal point of view the primary feature to be focused upon in the tradition is Onan's refusal. His action was condemned – the deity struck him down because of it. The circumstances and details of his action require careful assessment. He actually attempted intercourse with Tamar, but stopped short and spilled his seed on the ground. The reason for doing so was to conceal from his father,[27] at whose command he had gone into Tamar, his unwillingness to fulfil the levirate duty. If his father had known what was going on he would have dealt with him and, presumably, in the end ensured that he gave Tamar conception. As it was, condign punishment came from heaven: Onan – his name means the virile one – would not give life, so his was taken from him. But from Judah's point of view Onan's death had no such significance. Rather Tamar was the one to concentrate on: both his sons had died after a union with her, and his fear that if he commanded Shelah to go into her a similar fate might befall him, seems justified. Judah's resolve to enforce the levirate duty disappears.

The Deuteronomic law on the subject presupposes a more conventional situation. The father is simply not alive (although of interest, in light of the law's source of inspiration, it is not so stated), and hence the disappearance of that source of enforcement. A son's refusal in the absence of the father becomes the central element in the law, and because heaven cannot always be expected to act in such matters, the problem posed is how such a person might be dealt with for failing to do his duty.[28] It can be readily understood that with a positive duty of this kind compulsion is an unlikely instrument. The public authorities to whom the widow appeals – like Tamar she is a woman of initiative – can but try persuasion. If that fails the next step is to shame the man for his non-performance. This the widow proceeds to do. She draws off his sandal from his foot, and she spits in his face. The disgrace is not a passing, ephemeral thing. It will stick to the man from that time on, for his house ever after is named, 'The house of the drawn off sandal'. In a community sensitive to what people think of one another, to one's reputation, one's name – and Daube has brilliantly illuminated the strong shame-cultural element in the Deuteronomic laws[29] – such a sobriquet is designed to be damaging. Any *levir* who has no inclination to fulfil the levirate duty might well fear the disgrace of this kind of name-calling and reconsider. Such, presumably, is the point of the Deuteronomic law. The question is what inspired the two forms of disgrace, the removal of the sandal and the accompanying spitting, which the Deuteronomist incorporates into his law.

Onan's situation has provided the motivation and the particulars for this ceremony of disgrace. His sham action in avoiding his duty was contemptuously treated in the Genesis tradition. The offensive way in which he sought to give the appearance of granting conception to Tamar was met with his own extinction. Basically, his interruption of intercourse had the intention of refusing to give life to his dead brother's name. Despite his actions to the contrary, his purpose was not to perform on his behalf at all. His name is obviously an artificial Hebrew epithet designed to stigmatise his non-virile action. His name ever after will characterise his non-performance, his denial of conception to a woman.

In the Deuteronomic situation the living brother's offence is one of omission. In the face of his duty he remains passive, non-acting. He is like Onan. His non-action constitutes the denial of conception to the widow. To shame him for such non-performance the appropriate thing to do is to liken him even more to the proverbial Onan. His passiveness should be given contemptuous expression. Hence the drawing off of his sandal from his foot is intended to symbolise Onan's withdrawing from intercourse, a sandal being a symbol of the female genitals, and a foot, of the male sexual organ. The accompanying spitting symbolises Onan's spilling of the seed. The woman carries out these offensive gestures because she is telling him and the public bystanders that he is an Onan. His passiveness is no better, he is made to see, than Onan's sham actions. Moreover, ever after the name of his house, 'The house of the drawn off sandal', will convey to people the notion of conception denied, and hence his dishonourable failure to build up his dead brother's house. Even more precisely such a demeaning name is intended to recall his predecessor and his specific gesture of withdrawing from intercourse. Everyone in this society knows about him, his action was proverbial, his name was meant to recall it, and the woman's gestures, along with the name given to the man's house, are sufficient to brand him as an Onan.[30]

Needless to say, the meaning of the woman's gestures would be immediately recognised by the recipients of the law. All three, the sandal, the foot, and the spitting, bear sexual meanings in almost all cultures.[31] In biblical material spitting is used to indicate contempt,[32] but no other instance exists in which the contempt has a specific allusion to semen. It is not until post-biblical material that other specific examples of spittle in the sense of semen are found. There is one remarkable reference which shows that the view put forward here about the removal of the sandal as symbolic of intercourse, and the spitting, of semen, was similarly understood in some Rabbinic circles. Thus an isolated statement in *Sifre Deuteronomy* is attributed to Rabbi Ishmael: 'The removal is in lying down and the spitting is in implantation of seed.' [33]

Many examples exist in the Bible of the use of the word 'feet' in the sense of the genitals, male or female. [34] In Jacob's allusion to Judah's dilemma over the threatened extinction of his line he refers to the staff between the legs (*raglayim*, feet). [35] David's command to Uriah to go down to his house and 'wash his feet' bears the cryptic message that he should have intercourse with his wife. [36] The concealed meaning is all the more necessary in this example because David knows that it is contrary to custom for a soldier on active duty to enjoy conjugal relations. In fact the drama of the incident is enhanced by Uriah's strict observance of the custom. When the wife of Moses touched his 'feet' with their son's foreskin and exclaimed that he was a bridegroom of blood to her, the allusion is obviously to his own uncircumcised member. [37]

In the story of Ruth a sandal symbolises Ruth as the wife of the levirate union (it also coincidentally symbolises the right to tread on land for a legal purpose). [38] In a way that has not been hitherto recognised we shall see the importance this symbolism plays in the Ruth story. In that eulogy of earthly love, the Song of Songs, another form of the word for a sandal is found in an allusion to the bride. She is described as a 'locked garden' (*gan na'ul*). [39] The sexual overtone is unmistakable, the implication being that when the bridegroom steps foot into the garden he will have entered the bride.

The verb 'to draw off' (*ḥalaṣ*) in reference to the sandal indicates the intended sexual meaning of withdrawing from intercourse. In the story of Ruth, when the nearer kinsman takes off his sandal and hands it to Boaz in order to indicate the latter's right to redeem land, the verb is different (*šalap*). An excellent illustration of the sexual meaning of 'to draw off' is found in the application to God's relationship with Israel in Hosea 5:6. It has been one of husband and wife but the latter has strayed sexually, has actually produced children by other, illicit unions, and her true husband, God, has withdrawn from her. The reference is to the removal of his generative strength. A nominal ofrm of the word means a man's loins, and there are three instances in which the specific sense is virility, the place from which a man's sexual potency issues.[40] In the levirate ceremony of disgrace the woman draws off the man's sandal in order to suggest something about his virility, in particular, to mock him by comparing him to the 'virile' one, Onan, and his disengagement from intercourse with Tamar.

In light of his austere sexual morality it is likely that the Deuteronomist reacted strongly to Tamar's sexual initiative in waylaying Judah at Enaim, the more so in that the Genesis tradition is positive about it. He himself would certainly not encourage such initiative. What is remarkable, nonetheless, about his levirate law is the bold sexual symbolism that the woman is commanded to express in public. Albeit figuratively, she exposes a man's genitals. In the law that immediately follows, this particular sexual freedom on the part of a woman is put in true Deuteronomic perspective. He leaves the matter in no doubt whatever that such a freedom is narrowly circumscribed, confined to a strictly supervised area of concern, and in no way permitted in other areas of life, even where there might be some practical justification for it. Thus the law:

> When men fight with one another, and the wife of the one draws near to rescue her husband from the hand of him who is beating him, and puts out her hand and seizes him by the private parts, then thou shalt cut off her hands; thine eye shall have no pity.[41]

No law in biblical material carries such a specific mutilating penalty. It is perhaps a measure of the lawgiver's desire to ensure that no misunderstanding arises from his preceding permission to the levirate woman. That the law is in large measure prompted by the lawgiver's felt need to counteract any misconstruing of this permission would explain its surprising inclusion in the code.[42] The law confines itself to a case that by any reckoning would not have constituted a pressing legal problem.[43] Its existence provides another illustration of the Deuteronomic presentation of contrasting cases along the lines of wisdom instruction: it is wise and right to do one thing; it is foolish and wrong to do the other. Thus in the levirate law the woman's duty was to make a symbolic gesture in regard to the man's genitals. Contrariwise, the woman's action in interfering in the fight between the two men by grabbing the genitals of one of them is branded as crude and disgusting. The punishments also present an interesting contrast. In one case the offender, a male, has a foot exposed in public; in the other the offender, a female, has a hand cut off. It is to be noted that in each case the offender has caused no physical damage. In both instances the offence is one of disgrace: the male's constitutes one of omission, the female's one of commission.

The proverbial law in Deut 25:4 about not muzzling an ox in its treading is, like the law prohibiting an ox and an ass ploughing together, cryptic in character. Moreover, this cryptic element, again like the ox and ass law in relation to the laws that follow it and the Shechem story that has inspired them, has to do with the levirate law that follows the unmuzzled ox law and the Judah story that has inspired it. The presentation of the law against ploughing with an ox and an ass together was necessary in order to prepare the way for the Deuteronomist to use the tradition about Shechem's seduction of Dinah for Israelite legal purposes. Likewise, the Deuteronomist presents the law about the ox in order to use the Judah story for national purposes.

The meaning of the law is cleverly concealed. What is conveyed is the meaning and message of the following levirate law that an Israelite's name should not be blotted out in the land. An Israelite, the ox, should not be denied the fruits of his inheritance in the land, just as an ox should not be muzzled so that it is prevented from eating some of the grain, actually the first-fruits of the year's harvest, which it produces by its treading. The Deuteronomic legislation as a whole is concerned with Israel's inheritance of the land of Canaan, and the law in Deut 20:7 (supplemented by the similar law in 24:5) is particularly concerned with ensuring that an Israelite does not die (in war) before perpetuating his name by the birth of a child, and thereby guaranteeing the continuance of his inheritance. The levirate law concerns itself with the case in which an Israelite does die before perpetuating his name and lays down an extraordinary remedy for salvaging the situation. The law of the unmuzzled ox focuses attention on an Israelite's failure to grant the remedy and hence the law also has an unmistakable sexual meaning. Treading, like ploughing, is an allusion to intercourse,[44] and the reference is to the failure of an Israelite to carry on intercourse on behalf of his dead brother until a male heir is born.

There is in fact an integral connection between the two laws that refer to the ox figuratively. Apart from the similarity in meaning, and apart from the same use of animal imagery, there is also a clever play upon words that connects them. The word 'to plough' in Hebrew has the same consonants ($ḥrš$) as the word 'to be silent',[45] and hence the ploughing ox law has inspired the un-muzzled ox law in the sense that if one is referring to muzzling at the human level the notion revolves around the idea of silencing a person. In the levirate law an Israelite is silenced in three inter-related senses, by his death, by his lack of a male heir to continue his name, and by his brother's refusal to remedy this lack. It is no accident that the use of animal imagery and word-plays in the two laws about treading and ploughing recalls the characteristic features of the sayings by Jacob to his sons in Genesis 49. Both laws are intimately connected with two of the sayings, about Simeon and Levi and about Judah, because like them they relate to facts about the lives of Simeon and Levi in Genesis 34 and Judah in Genesis 38.

The law in Deut 22:10 is about an ox (an Israelite) and an ass (a Canaanite), while the law in Deut 25:4 is about an ox only. The point is that the latter law comes into being because the Deuter-onomist was working on the Judah story and noting the fact that Judah's three sons were in some sense Canaanites. The two who died, Er and Onan, are cryptically referred to as asses in Gen 49:11. As asses they were incongruously bound to the vine and proceeded to tread on it – such is the implication – and to destroy it. The allusion is to their sexual relationship with Tamar, which, ending in their deaths, threatened the continuation of Judah's line. The third son, Shelah, is not heard of again after Tamar's seduction of her father-in-law. The reason is that Judah, the son of an ox, perpetuated his name by giving conception himself, and not indirectly through his half-Canaanite sons. The implication is clear. For the authors of the Judah story in Genesis 38, the Judah saying in Gen 49:8–12, and the law in Deut 25:4, an ox should not be muzzled in its treading but an ass should (especially so if it is brought into contact with the Israelite vine). In other words, these authors believe that the death of the childless Er and Onan, and the casting aside of Shelah so that he would not be involved in produc-ing a child, was heaven's way of preventing a Canaanite infusion into the line of Israel, Judah's father.[46]

In using Er's situation to state the law on levirate marriage, the Deuteronomist, who was writing for national purposes, had to take account of the fact that Er was an ass, a Canaanite. The way in which he does so is by prefacing his law on the levirate custom with the law on the unmuzzled ox. His procedure is exactly analogous to his prefacing his law on the defamation of a virgin of Israel by a fellow-Israelite and the contrasting case where she has prostituted herself, with the law prohibiting an ox and an ass ploughing together. In regard to the Shechem story in Genesis 34, he had to expunge the Canaanite elements so that he could use its features to suggest matters of legal moment for the nation, Israel. The question raised in that discussion was why the Deuteronomist resorted to hidden meanings in stating the law on the ox and the ass. It was suggested that one factor was the need to blunt the criticism of Jacob who, from the Deuteronomic point of view, emerges none too well from the stance he took in the Shechem incident. A similar factor can be cited in the case of the law on the unmuzzled ox, only here it is Judah who is under critical scrutiny. Already in the narrative of Genesis 38 he is under attack for his treatment of Joseph. Probably the Deuteronomist, who agrees with this judgment on him,[47] is also very much opposed to his marriage to a Canaanite woman. Such opposition, however, in the Deuteronomist's time, in the very place, the land of Judah, which traced its history to the ancestor Judah, would probably have met with a hostile response in certain quarters. Hence the resort to a subtle, allusive law that justifies the continued existence of Judah's line but underneath hits out at him for his involvement with Canaanites.

RUTH

An understanding of the symbolism of the sandal and foot in the Deuteronomic levirate law enhances, in a way not hitherto realised, our appreciation of the Ruth story. Likewise, the cryptic content of the law about treading with an unmuzzled ox throws new light on the entire story. The scene to be discussed is the one in which Ruth, at Naomi's direction, visits Boaz at night, when he is lying down on his threshing floor, having winnowed his grain, and having eaten and drunk. The nature of this scene, far from being a matter of pure idyll and innocence,[1] is heavy with underlying sexual allusion. Any reader, ancient or modern, cannot but be aware of its suppressed meaning and, precisely on this account, is compelled to probe it. In other words, part of the intention of the story-teller is to invite his hearers to go along with his allusiveness and to await its unveiling, which does indeed come in the scene at the city gate the following day.

In an introduction to the scene we learn that Naomi is anxious to secure a home, literally, a resting-place, for Ruth. She means, although she does not say it, a husband. Her directions are precise. With her best clothes on, and suitably anointed, Ruth has to seek Boaz out at his threshing place and there, only after he has attained a pleasant state of rest because he has completed his agricultural work and enjoyed some food and drink, has she to expose his feet and lie down. No less than four times do we hear about the related activities of lying down and uncovering the male's feet. Such repetition urges the reader to be perceptive.

The clue is the figurative sense of 'sandal' and 'feet'. When Ruth exposes Boaz's feet the intention is to suggest the uncovering of his genital region because of the already noted, widely attested, sexual meaning of 'feet'. She, in turn, is offering herself as his new shoes or sandals because of the sexual significance of the sandal as the female genitalia. Ruth's actions are intended to speak for themselves, but to declare a meaning other than their literal one. When she does speak, at the time when Boaz awakens from his rest and finds her at his feet, her language too is figurative. She requests him to spread his skirt over her. The text in Ezek 16:8,[2] even though the reference is to the deity as a human lover, makes it clear that Ruth is asking Boaz to be her husband. Understood figuratively, her request is synonymous with her action in regard to lying at his feet. Boaz is asked, it is implied, to remove his garment and put it upon her. If this action were carried out he would uncover himself and, similar to the situation described in Ezekiel, cover her nakedness with it. The intended meaning is that Ruth will, in turn, become his new garment or skirt. He is to put her on as his skirt, that is, as his wife, just as in the preceding action on the threshing floor the removal of his shoes was to the end that he might put on a new pair, Ruth as wife. There can be little doubt that the reference in the Deuteronomic law to a man's wife as his skirt is attributable to this figurative, proverbial language of love and betrothal.[3]

What is remarkable about the description of this scene is the symbolism that is suggested by each little detail, whether in language or action. Even Naomi's desire to obtain for Ruth a place or state of rest in the oblique sense of having her married to a man is worked out in a similarly oblique way in terms of the actions on the threshing floor; Ruth's lying down at the place of Boaz's feet (so the Hebrew expression, *marg^{e}lot*, in Ruth 3:4), he already in a state of rest in a plain sense. The major symbolic feature, however, because of the setting of the scene at the threshing floor, belongs to the figurative notions associated with treading or threshing.

We have already seen with respect to the Deuteronomic levirate law and the law that precedes and introduces it, 'Thou shalt not muzzle an ox in its treading', that treading, like ploughing, can refer to intercourse.[4] To tread with the feet by putting on shoes gives this figurative sense.[5] Underlying the meaning and intention of the law is the idea that an Israelite, the ox, should step into his dead brother's 'shoes', and by treading should produce 'first-fruits' for his deceased, childless brother. That way, the dead brother, the fellow-Israelite ox, will in fact not have been muzzled in his treading, which up to the point of his death had produced no first-fruits in the sense of human offspring. The inheritance law in Deut 21:17 speaks of a first-born son as the first-fruits of a man's strength, an expression which derives its origin from this agricultural background. One factor which must have contributed to the proverb about the unmuzzled ox is that its activity produces the very first new grain from the harvest, truly its first-fruits.

Boaz is a successful farmer who, having harvested his grain, has taken it to his threshing floor, threshed, and winnowed it. He then enjoys some food, some drink, and lies down in a mood of merriness induced by the drink beside his freshly threshed heap of grain. It is at this point that a woman, who is designated time and again as a Moabitess, uncovers his feet, lies down beside them, and requests the startled male to spread his skirt over her, 'for thou art next of kin'. In tradition (Lot and his daughters in Gen 19:30–8), a Moabitess without a child would be proverbially thought of as someone who might lie with her nearest kinsman when he is in a drunken state. In the Ruth story the combination of activities, circumstances, and setting carries the suggestion that Boaz should now proceed to do some treading – in the sexual sense, with Ruth as his footwear. Boaz is agreeable, but because he is not in fact the nearest kinsman he wishes such a step to be postponed until the entire matter is taken up publicly.

In the meantime he keeps Ruth overnight with him, at his feet, on the threshing floor. In the morning she returns, unbeknown to any outsider, with six measures of barley in her possession as a gift from Boaz to Naomi. The latter, who has masterminded the whole affair, understands the meaning of this gesture. The forthcoming union of Boaz with Ruth, to be followed by the production of first-fruits, in the transferred sense of human offspring, is anticipated. Ruth will have proved herself worth more than seven sons to Naomi, but in particular the first son to be born of her union with Boaz will be reckoned to Naomi.[6]

An interesting detail in the narrative supports the connection between agricultural and human first-fruits. After her night spent at the threshing floor Boaz places the six measures of his new grain, the first-fruits of his harvest, in the folds of the garment that is around her waist. The picture conveyed is that of a woman bearing a burden in a way that suggests a woman carrying an unborn child.[7] The link is made clearer by observing that when Ruth's first child is eventually born it was laid in Naomi's bosom. The same verb, *šit*, is used for the placing in Ruth's lap of the grain that is to be taken to Naomi, and also for the laying of the child in the latter's lap.

What took place at Boaz's threshing floor was of a private nature with symbolic, sexual language and action appropriate to such a context. What takes place the next day at the city gate is public in character and is more concerned with plain language and action. However, symbolism is also introduced and it serves as a link to the symbolic meaning of the night before.

Boaz calls the nameless first kinsman before an assembly of town elders, informs him that Naomi is selling the parcel of land that belonged to his relative, Elimelech, and asks him if he is prepared to redeem it. He responds positively. But when he is informed that with the land must also come the duty of raising up the name of the dead, he withdraws all interest in land and marriage. As a reason, he cites the ruin of his own inheritance should he take on the duty to perpetuate Elimelech's. Boaz, as the next kinsman, now declares his willingness to redeem the land, and to raise seed for Elimelech by taking on Ruth as his wife. To transfer this right of redemption to Boaz the first kinsman removes his sandal and, either actually or by implication, hands it to Boaz.

It has to be explained to the readers of the story that this gesture is of a symbolic, legal nature. They no longer knew that in times past a sandal was used this way in legal transactions.[8] Before the elders and the public bystanders Boaz declares what has transpired. He has acquired the right to redeem Elimelech's piece of land and he has purchased Ruth to be his wife, 'to raise up the name of the dead upon his inheritance'. For the readers of the story a sandal has now two symbolic associations: an action involving the transfer of some land and an action involving a woman. What must catch their attention is the way in which these two actions cannot be separated. Indeed, the intention of the story is to reveal this link between the one and the other. For, to state the matter plainly, the purpose of redeeming the land is that it will become the property of Elimelech's heir. He, however, does not yet exist. Only when a child is conceived by Ruth will Elimelech's inheritance be guaranteed. The literal and transferred sense of treading brings out this sought for unity of intention. When Boaz treads out Ruth by going into her, as he eventually does,[9] the male child born, Obed as it turns out, will in due course tread Elimelech's piece of land as its owner. The 'first-fruits' of the threshing accomplished by Boaz with Ruth will lead to the renewed production of the first-fruits of Elimelech's fields. The first redeemer's failure to take Ruth represents the refusal to recognise that Elimelech's land should continue to have his name attached to it. His spurning his duty results in his own name going unrecorded in history.

The importance of what treading stands for in the book of Ruth cannot be over-estimated. Elimelech and his family are from Bethlehem, the place of bread. The name implies that successful grain harvests are associated with it. Elimelech had himself pro-

duced two sons in this place.[10] His fertility is linked with that of
Bethlehem, and the designation of himself and his family as
Ephrathites further underlines this implicit theme, because that
name seems to refer also to the notion of fruitfulness.[11] Alas, fate
interferes with all that Bethlehem stands for. A famine strikes and
Elimelech and his family have to leave. They go to the neighbour-
ing country of Moab. This place-name too is resonant with associations, but this time undesirable ones.

Moab is linked by tradition – so Genesis 19 – with the dearth of
child-producing males. It was this lack that prompted Lot's elder
daughter to become pregnant by her father, the name Moab ('from
father') being a reference to her dubious initiative in these circumstances. The deaths of Elimelech and his two married but childless
sons fit, or are made to fit,[12] the bitter fate that the first Moabite
woman lamented. Both Mahlon and Chilion were Judeans but the
point is that they were living in Moab. The fact that Ruth was
eventually to prove herself fertile *in Judah* raises the question why
neither she nor Orpah had been able to conceive in Moab.[13] Its
proverbial association with the problem of obtaining progeny in the
natural way of things explains this puzzle. For Naomi, Ruth, and
Orpah no treading male exists to produce offspring for this family.
The loss of agricultural treading in Bethlehem is complemented by
the loss of human treading in Moab. The clever interplay between
theme and geographical location is quite pronounced.

The link between the two types of treading re-emerges when
Naomi hears that there is again food available back home. Her
decision to return brings in its wake her concern that her two
daughters-in-law might find husbands, and achieve the security of
a home and family life. It is as if the resumption of harvests back in
Bethlehem and the subsequent process of threshing bring to her
mind the needs of her daughters-in-law for treading males. When
Ruth and Orpah respond negatively to her well-intentioned direction that they remain in Moab to find husbands, and request instead
that they accompany her back to Bethlehem, Naomi's response is in
terms of what she considers impossible of fulfilment, because of her
age, namely, an application of the levirate custom. We have already
seen that it is this custom which brings together human and
agricultural treading. An Israelite should not be muzzled in his
treading, that is, denied the first-fruits of land and family. Orpah,
having started out on the journey to Judah, returns to Moab. Ruth
attaches herself to Naomi. The two of them go to Bethlehem and,

significantly, it is the beginning of the barley harvest there.

S. Bertman has shown how the author of the book of Ruth has designed his composition.[14] For example, the book begins and ends with genealogical information. Or, again, the description of events concerning Ruth in the fields of Boaz (chapter two) is observed to inspire a symmetrical description of events concerning Ruth at Boaz's threshing floor (chapter three). His observations are convincing. But rather than stop at the literary connections between these two agricultural scenes we can go further and observe a fundamental link in meaning that ties them together. Crucial in this connection is the very real crux of how Naomi in the time of transition between the two scenes comes up with the bizarre, detailed instructions to Ruth about paying a visit to Boaz's threshing-floor. Recall that she has to dress up, wait until he has eaten and drunk, make herself known to him when he is lying down on his threshing-floor, uncover his feet, and lie beside him. This response, so heavily laden with meaning, is intended to elicit an appropriately meaningful response from Boaz. Where is such meaning coming from ? The answer lies in the significance that Naomi reads into the events of the gleaning in Boaz's fields. It is by chance, and chance frequently arouses curiosity about wider significance, that Ruth finds herself gleaning in Boaz's field. He is particularly well disposed to her, is especially solicitous of her welfare, and encourages her to take grain over and above what the activity of gleaning allows. By a process akin to threshing Ruth beats out one full measure of grain and takes it back to Naomi, along with some grain which she had been given at mealtime and which had proved more than adequate for her needs.

Naomi interprets these events. In a way she is the author's foil in the working out of his story. Already in regard to her life, first in Bethlehem, then in Moab and her return to Bethlehem, she had thought that a change of name from Naomi, 'pleasant life', to Mara, 'bitter-fated', characterised the events of her previous existence. Now she undertakes the interpretation of how things are falling out for her because of her companion in adversity, Ruth.

Three facets of her interpretation might be noted. First, in her response to Ruth and Orpah about the problem of their future security she had touched on the possibility, really for the purpose of dismissing it, of a remedy through an application of the levirate custom. That custom requires the initiative of a male kinsman. Ruth happens to find herself gleaning in the field of a kinsman of

Elimelech's family, Boaz. To be sure, although he is generous to her and acknowledges what has happened to Elimelech's family, he makes no move to recognise any levirate duty in regard to his kinsman. The evidence of the Judah-Tamar story, even of the story of Lot and his daughters, of the Deuteronomic levirate law, and now of the story of Ruth, is that male initiative in furthering a family line could be notoriously lacking. Nonetheless, Naomi regards the encounter between Ruth and the kinsman, Boaz, as something to be reflected upon in the context of the levirate custom.

Secondly, the fact that eventually Naomi sends Ruth to Boaz's threshing-floor and instructs her not to proceed with certain actions until after he has eaten and drunk, to the extent of his being merry, further underlines the point that male kinsmen were not exactly rushing to do their duty on behalf of a dead relative. In other words, the approach to the male only when he is in a congenial mood suggests that an approach at another time might meet with a negative response. Still, one wonders further about this specific direction. Strictly, its import is to wait until Boaz has eaten and drunk; in the carrying out of it Ruth waits until he has done that and 'his heart is merry'. Time and time again in the story, the name Ruth is followed by the designation, the Moabitess. Surely Naomi's direction has not just to do with the problem of making a male kinsman open to the suggestion of thinking about the levirate custom. It has also to do with her recognising that in the present circumstances Ruth's Moabite background need not be a disadvantage but, on the contrary, something to be used to good effect. If good fortune had favoured Ruth's encounter with a male who was a kinsman of Elimelech, then the same good fortune might bring about a present-day Moabitess achieving what her first ancestress achieved. The latter, we recall, was faced with the prospect of no future progeny for her father's line and remedied the problem by her use of wine. How coincidental, if in a less crude and more subtly suggestive way, that Ruth the Moabitess approaches a kinsman about the matter of progeny after he is through with his potations. Naomi switches from associating Moab with loss to associating it with gain.

The third factor that inspires Naomi to take control of events is her natural acquaintance with the symbolism that is associated with the completion of the year's harvest. This symbolism, in different guises, is known to almost all cultures, ancient and

modern.[15] The particular significance which Naomi pursues is
therefore not an isolated and unexpected quirk of the imagination.
When Boaz, Elimelech's kinsman, treats Ruth with acts of kind-
ness Naomi fits them into the context of the levirate custom. He had
supplied her with food, parched grain, at a work-break, more than
enough in fact, so that she was able to keep some aside for taking
back to Naomi. This provision of prepared grain signifies that food
is available for her again in Bethlehem, which was her reason for
returning home. Originally, food in Bethlehem and the blessing of
family life, the fertility of successful treading in field and womb,
expressed Naomi's lot in life. Boaz had further supplied grain to
Ruth out of his current crop. This supply had required Ruth to
engage in a process that was comparable to threshing.[16] It was this
act, which produced one full measure of grain, which preceded
Boaz's own work of threshing, that suggests to Naomi that such
mutual activity by Ruth and Boaz might be complemented at the
human level. Threshing, we noted, has that sexual overtone, just
as the production of grain, especially the newly threshed, can
suggest human first-fruits.

All of the above factors make it intelligible why Naomi gives
Ruth her extraordinary instructions for visiting Boaz, after the
completion of his agricultural threshing. Moreover, it is clear that
the various meanings of treading are woven into the entire story
and contribute to its unity of composition. There is treading in the
ordinary sense of moving about on foot. That might seem an
unremarkable and inevitable aspect of almost any story in which
journeying of one kind or another occurs. But even in this regard
there is sometimes an undue emphasis that is baffling without some
such explanation as is suggested here. What is one to make, for
example, of the strange fact that Naomi, Ruth, and Orpah all set
out on the way to Bethlehem *before* Naomi urges them to remain on
their home territory?[17] Or, consider the heaping up of verbs to do
with treading, 'to go forth', 'to return', 'to go', in this particular
section of material.[18] Or, the similar accumulation in the incident
involving Ruth's initiative to go and glean in the fields, and which
leads to the coming together for the first time of Ruth and Boaz.
'Let me go to the field and glean', says Ruth, and Naomi tells her,
'Go, my daughter'. 'So she set forth and went.' Shortly, 'Boaz came
from Bethlehem'. He asks about Ruth and is told that she is the
Moabitess, 'who came back with Naomi from the country of
[literally the fields of] Moab'. Some statistics may be revealing. In

the relatively brief compass of the story the verb *halak* occurs some eighteen times, *bo'* eighteen times, *šub* fifteen times.[19]

An illuminating parallel to the treading that Ruth invites Boaz to think about when he is lying down on his threshing-floor is provided by the Song of Songs. This work, which throughout depicts scenes of love-making, contains a description of the attributes of the bride as seen through the eyes of the bridegroom.[20] 'How beautiful are thy feet in sandals', he exclaims. He is hinting at more than what his eyes see. He is thinking of the time when his own 'feet' will be adorned with her 'sandals', and he can tread her. This anticipation of forthcoming pleasures is why he goes on immediately to describe her genital region (without any intervening reference to parts of the body in between): her thighs, her navel and her belly. The latter he likens to a heap of wheat surrounded by lilies. The lilies refer to the pubic hair[21] and the wheat to the place where his treading produces seed. The allusion enhances our understanding of the detail in the Ruth story about Boaz's lying down beside the heap of grain. It was there that Ruth removed his shoes to uncover his feet and to lie down beside him. We also recall how at the conclusion of this scene Boaz had heaped up grain in Ruth's lap. We are meant to see that eventually his treading will make her pregnant. In post-biblical Hebrew, 'the threshing place' (*meqom dišah*) is (figuratively): 'The place where the male organ carries out intercourse, that is, the female genitals.'[22]

Finally, treading in the Book of Ruth is also used in a legal sense. In times past, its readers are informed, in legal matters, when a man drew off his sandal and handed it to another, the effect was to confirm an act of redemption or one of exchange. The ritual seems to have covered many things. Originally, it would appear, it had a particular application in regard to the conveyance of immovable objects such as houses or land. Where no written document was used and an object was too large or inappropriate for handing over to a person in front of witnesses, stepping on the object in question, into the house, or upon the land, with the buyer's using a sandal provided for the occasion by the seller, constituted a formal act of conveyance. The treading in Ruth concerns some land.[23]

So far we have sought to uncover some hitherto unrecognised cultural ideas and assumptions that underlie the Book of Ruth and which, if they are in any way accurate, throw new light on the author's meaning. Another aim has been to reveal certain connections that exist between his work and other biblical material. This comparative study can be greatly extended. It is prompted by the observation that the problem of obtaining progeny to continue a male line is the one feature shared by the story of Lot and his daughters, the story of Judah and Tamar, the Deuteronomic levirate law, and the story of Ruth. We have already shown that the traditions about Lot and Judah have received the attention of the Deuteronomic lawgiver. The latter's concern, for example, with the absence of the enforcing authority of a father has stemmed from his scrutiny of the Judah-Tamar story. It remains to demonstrate that this same story has subtly influenced the composition of the Book of Ruth.

The role of the tradition about Lot in the story of Ruth has been commented upon at length in the above discussion. One other link remains to be seen. A feature of the Ruth story is the emphasis upon the gap in age between Ruth and Boaz. At one point, for example, he thanks her for not pursuing young men,[24] the implication being that she has turned to him instead and that he is of an older generation. Lot, of course, is one generation removed from his daughter. It happens, however, that this feature of the age difference is also present in the story of Judah: Tamar decides to become pregnant by her father-in-law instead of by Shelah, Judah's remaining son. It is, therefore, difficult to evaluate how one should view this element in the story of Ruth, whether to relate it to one tradition or to both. In some respects the link might be drawn more closely to the Judah tradition.

Ruth and the Judah-Tamar Tradition. Unlike the Moabite tradition, the one about Judah and Tamar is explicitly cited in Ruth 4:12: 'May thine house', declare the assembled people and elders at the gate to Boaz, 'be like the house of Perez, whom Tamar bore to Judah, because of the children that the Lord will give thee by this young woman.' The house to be established by the birth of children to Boaz and Ruth is compared to the house of Perez, the male child born to Judah and Tamar. One should not read too much into this comparison. Only Perez and his twin were born to them because we learn that Judah had no further relations with her.[25] Many children are to be born to Boaz and Ruth. There seems no reason to expect specific comparisons between Judah and Boaz, on the one hand, and Tamar and Ruth, on the other; just as the comparison of Ruth to Rachel and Leah in 4:11 does not suggest anything other than the notion of each woman bringing forth children for the building up of the one male line of Israel.

Are there, however, comparisons to be made which can only be explained by the influence of the Judah story upon the Ruth story? This seems highly probable when one looks in on the puzzling role of the unnamed kinsman who is a nearer relative to Elimelech than Boaz. No approach had been made to have him do his duty by his deceased relative. Yet Naomi must have known of his existence. When it is recalled that Naomi only has Ruth approach Boaz when he is in a state of well-being induced by food and drink, the avoidance of the nearer kinsman also suggests the underlying social difficulty of having a relative fulfil his levirate obligation. The assumption is that Naomi ignored a plea to him because she anticipated a negative response. After all, what stands out in regard to both this man and Boaz is their inactivity in fulfilling a duty which is primarily, if not wholly, that of the male.

There is evidence that this nearer kinsman is drawn in a much poorer light than meets the eye, a feature that need not occasion surprise because of the book's characteristic allusiveness. In a word, he is likened to the infamous Onan. Thus both he and Onan wanted for themselves the available estates of Er and Elimelech respectively.[26] They did not wish to provide heirs for their kinsmen. The nearer kinsman's outright refusal to take Ruth is comparable to Onan's having interrupted intercourse with Tamar insofar as both are set on denying conception to the widow. Interesting in this regard is the possibility that the nearer kinsman's removal of his sandal, apart from its legal significance, may be intended to be seen also as unwitting self-mockery on his part because of the sexual symbolism associated with a sandal. His denial of conception is likened to Onan's spurning of Tamar during intercourse.

A further link with Onan is to be seen in one of the book's most puzzling linguistic features. While it is not surprising that the nearer kinsman is given no name – he refused to perpetuate Elimelech's name, so his own name is treated as unimportant – what is surprising is Boaz's reference to him as *pᵉloni 'almoni* 'such and such a one'. As applied by Boaz it is without parallel in biblical literature.[27] He uses it on the occasion of his calling the kinsman before the city gate. It is clear, however, that the author is not reporting direct speech but is substituting this expression for the man's original name. E.F. Campbell details a large number of instances in which the author, through assonance, indulges in word-plays.[28] He does not cite one in this instance. Yet the doubly repeated *'on* sound is a prominent feature of this expression. In that Onan (*'onan*) has a proverbial reputation in the levirate context, in that the book of Ruth actually reminds its readers of the story in which he was involved, and in that his name mockingly refers to his virility (*'on*), it would appear that the author has chosen the expression *pᵉloni 'almoni* because there can be picked up from it an allusion to Onan, or at least to the matter of virility which is about to come up.[29]

Another puzzle that may be solved by noting the author's comparison of the nearer kinsman to Onan is the assertion attributed to him that, should he take the wife of the dead for the purpose of raising up the name of the deceased upon his inheritance, he would destroy his own. A great deal has been written about the meaning of his statement. A common view is that he already possesses a wife and children, and the financial burden of taking on another wife and child would be too great for him. His own inheritance would then be threatened with disarray, marred in some sense, as most of the translations put it. But an existing marriage is not even implied, and this view greatly attenuates the meaning of the verb *hišḥit*, 'to destroy'.[30] Another view is taken by W.O.E.Oesterley and T.H.Robinson who assume that monogamy was the rule at the time in question.[31] From this perspective, they think they are able to provide the satisfactory solution that the man will be unable to perpetuate his own family line if he commits himself to marrying Ruth. This assumes, however, that a second child born to them could not become heir to his own estate. There is no basis for such an assumption. More recently, D.Daube has also argued for this solution to the problem, but he introduces the subtlety that the nearer kinsman understood the reference to the 'wife of the dead' as alluding to Naomi only. The kinsman therefore reckoned that while Naomi might just produce one child, it was most unlikely that she would produce a second one who would become heir to his property. Hence he declines to fulfil his duty and Boaz, who by his deliberately deceptive use of the expression 'wife of the dead' had hoped for this negative response, is then able to take the other wife of the dead, Ruth.[32]

There is, however, no evidence for a monogamous rule at such an early stage in Israelite history.[33] Moreover, on the basis of such a view, the man's motivation in declining to marry the widow is not without merit. He is as justified in seeking to perpetuate his own family line as is a fellow Israelite (through a surviving relative) in pressing the claim of the levirate obligation. A similar motivation underlies each position. Only the existence of a rule of monogamy, over which they have no control, prevents a mutually satisfactory arrangement. The attention given to the nearer kinsman in the story would then seem hardly worthwhile and no aura of disgrace would attach to him for his decision.

A way out of the difficulty is to see a subtle attempt on the part of the author to portray the nearer kinsman as a sort of Onan. He has already done this by slipping into the mouth of Boaz the designation of him as *peloni 'almoni*. He does it again by having the man speak much too dramatically about what would happen if he took the widow. If polygamy is permitted, or even if the first child of the union becomes heir to Elimelech's estate and a second child heir to his own, then he should not speak about destroying his patrimony. He may burden himself, although even that is far from necessarily being the case.[34] The author is having him speak this way because he is being made to confess the fact that should he take her he might be tempted to do what Onan did with Tamar, and, as a consequence, meet Onan's fate. He would avoid giving her conception because his material desires would wish him to acquire Elimelech's estate for all time. But if his greed overcame him and he withheld conception, he knew, what everyone knew, that a predecessor in that kind of situation became undone, losing his life and two inheritances, his dead brother's and his own. In linking the nearer kinsman to Onan along this line of reasoning, there is one favourable piece of evidence. Onan destroyed (*šiḥet*) his seed.[35] The nearer kinsman, in refusing to take the widow for the purpose of granting her conception, had reasoned, 'lest I destroy my own inheritance' (*hišḥit*). In giving of his seed to her he might be tempted to waste it, thereby endangering himself, and threatening the destruction of his own inheritance.

It is Boaz who eventually takes Ruth and gives her conception. There is some ground for believing that personal names in the book are intended to convey meaning that is pertinent to the circumstances described in the story. If so, the name Boaz, which seems to allude to the notion of strength, even manly vigour,[36] would reflect the same kind of meaning, only in a positive sense, to be found in the name Onan.

There is an interesting trend discernible when we move from the stories of Lot's daughters and Judah-Tamar to the story of Ruth, then to the Deuteronomic levirate law. A greater sense of propriety prevails when we compare the Ruth story with the two Genesis traditions, and an even greater one when we compare the law with all three stories. Even in comparing the Judah-Tamar story with that of Lot's daughters there is already a concern, or at least the issue is raised, with the correctness of the sexual initiative undertaken by Tamar, in contrast to the apparently neutral attitude to the initiative of Lot's daughters. Tamar's action is said by Judah to be a justified one because he had denied her the proper means of obtaining a child to continue her dead husband's name.

We have already noted, in comparing Ruth's action with her ancestress's, that she waits until the male is merry with wine whereas Lot's daughter deliberately supplied him with it for the purpose of removing his inhibitions. Ruth proceeds to suggest to Boaz that he might seek a union with her, a suggestion that is taken up but is not acted upon immediately. Her Moabite ancestress, on the other hand, lay there and then with her father. Ruth's activity, as well as the context in which it takes place, is but a distinct echo of the original activity of the progenitress of her race. For one who reflects upon the difference, as presumably the author of Ruth did, Ruth's action can pass as justified, if somewhat daring and sailing close to the wind, in a way that cannot be said of the action of Lot's daughter. After all, her Israelite mother-in-law directed it initially.

If Ruth in muted fashion behaves according to her background and origin, the same is true of Tamar. Her designation as a sacred prostitute (*qᵉdešah*) is significant when we ask why she chose to prostitute herself with Judah as her remedy for obtaining a child. Although it is not stated, she is probably, like Judah's wife, a Canaanite, and sacred prostitution is a feature of that culture and religion.[37] Tamar's link with her background is far from being made explicit and this may be because the author of the story wishes to suppress as much as possible the fact that she is the Canaanite mother of Judah's line. From indications within the story, from the related saying in Genesis 49, and from its position in the Book of Genesis, the intention of the story is to undo any Canaanite influence on Jacob's family line. The reference to Judah's not lying with her again also suggests the minimising of this influence. It is probable that the author of the Ruth story has noted such features in the Tamar story and incorporated them into his own tale. Thus although he makes clear Ruth's Moabite background, he downplays it in two ways. He has, as just noted, made her act as a shadow of her ancestress, in fact to some extent as a contrasting one; and he goes out of his way to record that Ruth sought to leave her Moabite origins altogether: she would devote herself to the Judean god and she wished to be buried in the land of Judea.[38] Her dubious background unlike Tamar's is made explicit, but like Tamar she deals with it in such a way that her worth is proved in her relationship with a Judean.

Both Tamar and Ruth made their sexual advances at a time of festivity in the agricultural year. On Judah's way to a sheep-shearing event Tamar seduced him and at the end of the threshing process Ruth offered herself to Boaz.[39] Up to a certain point each acts in character, one as a sacred prostitute whose calling actually requires a state of constant infertility,[40] the other as a Moabitess whose lack of child-bearing capacity can be linked to her national origin. Their infertility revealed itself in their apparently death-possessing qualities. Tamar was told to remain away (as a widow in her father's house) because death in Judah's family is associated with her: two sons had died after intercourse with her. Her fatal influence was in fact only apparent, but it is sustained and heightened as the story develops: death threatens her, precisely because of her intercourse with Judah. If her death had occurred, her infertility would have been sustained and she would have remained true to her original sacred calling. The fact that she actively sought to procreate implies that she wished to break from her background. This feature comes much more into the open in the case of Ruth and again may be reckoned as inspiring it.

Ruth, in turn, was told to remain behind in Moab because death in Elimelech's family was, albeit in part only, associated with her. She proves to be fertile in Judah, but it is to be inferred that had she remained in Moab she would have continued to be infertile. Both women's procreative activity is eventually successful, but there is again a contrast which reveals more propriety in Ruth's action than in Tamar's. Tamar disguised herself from Judah in a public place in order to seduce him; Ruth made herself known to Boaz in a private place with a view to suggesting a proper time when she might conceive by him.

In Tamar and Ruth's association with Judeans all sorts of parallel symbolic acts and meanings come out. Tamar put off her garments of widowhood and veiled herself as a prostitute before Judah. Her aim was to acquire a child by him. She came into possession of his staff and was to hold it until such time as Judah delivered a new-born kid of his flock.[41] But she had also possessed his staff in a sexual sense,[42] and instead of receiving the kid she was delivered of a son, Judah's. Ruth suggested to Boaz that she become his new garment and new shoes, both in the sexual sense. His gifts of grain to her for Naomi indicated that new harvests were again available for Elimelech's family in Bethlehem. But they also pointed forward to the successful sexual treading which Boaz would accomplish with Ruth, and which would provide the renewal of first-fruits, in the human sense, for Elimelech's line. This successful treading contrasted with the earlier destruction of the latter's two married Judean sons in Moab after they had departed to that country because of the lack of agricultural activity in Bethlehem. Jacob's wry view of the deaths of Judah's two sons, Er and Onan, was that (Canaanite) asses should not have trodden the Israelite (Judean) vine.[43] This is how he explains their destruction; in treading the vine they had trampled upon it,[44] with the result that they themselves had been destroyed.

How many of these parallel features are to be explained because of a general community of subject matter and how many because the earlier Judah story has inspired the author of Ruth can remain open. What is sometimes implicit in the former is made explicit in the latter. Contrariwise, in the interests of refinement and propriety, there is a reaction against the explicit sexual features in the former with a movement towards a more subtle and suppressed presentation in the latter. In this respect, Boaz contrasts with Judah, his ancestor. The latter lay with Tamar when she used her sexuality in a public place to compromise him. He never lay with her again. Boaz in a similarly compromising situation, but in a private place, did not lie with Ruth; instead he attended to things properly and took her as a wife. In the Genesis story Shelah was not sent into Tamar. Judah's fear was that his fate might be that of Onan. This would mean, in actuality, that he might be tempted to do what Onan did. The nearer kinsman's role in the Ruth story is structurally parallel to Onan's. The result is that he is subtly depicted as fearing that he might be tempted to do what Onan did. He refrains from going into Ruth. In sketching the parallel with him, however, the author of Ruth proceeds in a muted, allusive fashion. The contrast reveals the always interesting and perennial concern with striking a balance between crudity and refinement, the obtrusive and the unobtrusive, substance and show. What is reported realistically in an earlier time is either covered over or given a psychological attribution in a later.

Ruth and the Deuteronomic Levirate Law. The difficulty of dating
material should never be underestimated and the evidence that the
Deuteronomic levirate law is later than the Ruth story is not con-
clusive. The indications that it is are nonetheless persuasive.
Recent research has come out strongly in favour of a much earlier
date, in fact a predeuteronomic one, for the Book of Ruth, which is
contrary to a widely held previous view.[45] The deuteronomic law
prohibiting for all time any access to the Israelite 'assembly of the
Lord' for Ammonites and Moabites appears to reflect a later,
totally negative attitude to these two groups from that which is
found (for the Moabites) in the Ruth story.[46] Both law and
narrative work with the tradition in Gen 19:30–38 about Moabite
and Ammonite origins. The Ruth narrative reveals an interesting
attempt to undo the taint of her ancestry by a process of *imitation
par opposition*,[47] which enables her to achieve a position of worth
in her relationship to one family within the Israelite community.
The Deuteronomist is equally aware of, in our terms, the genetic
influence of the Moabites' origin but his response is the opposite
of that in the Ruth story. He looks for a fault in every generation of
the Moabites and finds it, for example, in the one belonging to the
particular period of history he is speaking out of.[48] This Israelite
nationalistic attitude is likely to be later than the pre-nationalistic
one that emerges in the Ruth story.

The major feature of the Deuteronomic laws is their immersion
in the problems and trends to be found in existing traditions. Just
as the Ruth composition is acquainted with the Tamar tradition so
the Deuteronomist is probably acquainted with both. His levirate
law represents a negative response to the female procreative
initiative that is found in both the Tamar and Ruth traditions. If
the male is unwilling to fulfil the levirate duty, the widow is not to
resort to trickery or intrigue in trying to cajole him into conformity.
Self-help on her part is ruled out. The public authorities are to be
involved and if their persuasion is unsuccessful a public ceremony
of disgrace is to be administered by the widow against the disloyal
levir. But there the matter is to end. The Deuteronomist is particularly sensitive about the propriety of the woman's public action, as
the law about the immodest woman, which takes up from the preceding levirate law, demonstrates. This concern with refinement
is a reaction against the kind of activity the women undertake in
both the Tamar and Ruth traditions. But it is also a step beyond
the measure of propriety that has entered the Ruth story (because

of its author's attempt to avoid the more explicit features of the Tamar story).

This same process of increasing sensitivity about actions recorded in past traditions has already been commented upon in regard to the Genesis traditions about Abraham's treatment of Sarah with the pharaoh, his treatment of her with Abimelech, and Isaac's treatment of Rebecca with Abimelech. More and more concern with preserving the matriarch's virtue entered into these narratives. The culmination of the process came with certain Deuteronomic laws that took up the problems raised in these traditions.

Kingship in Ruth. The setting of the Book of Ruth in the period of the Judges suggests that the major change from the kind of government characteristic of that period to a monarchical one may be pertinent to the changes in fortune experienced by the family of Elimelech. The name of the head of this family clearly proclaims the meaning, 'My God is King' (*'elimelek*).[49] He lives but three generations before David becomes king, that is, at the beginning of this transition. What is more, as the end of the story brings out, Elimelech's family produces the royal line of David. Some interesting points can be raised about the possible relevance of this development, one that is acknowledged by the opening and closing statements of the book,[50] to an understanding of the reasons underlying its composition.

The family whose name expressed loyalty to God as king almost disappeared. They left Judah, and the males all died. What happened to them is symbolic of those families who supported the *status quo*: they had become a minority and were losing out to those who sought to establish kingship after the fashion of the surrounding nations. Their minority view had been expressed in a fable which equated the movement toward kingship with seeking the barren rule of the bramble, and the *status quo*, the maintenance of the independence of the landowning classes, with the fruit-bearing olive, vine, and fig.[51] Alas, the fortunes of Elimelech's family became synonymous with famine in Judah and appeared to reflect the exact opposite of that expressed in the fable.

One of the arguments for having a human king may have been that in a time of famine the type of government he represented could provide a central administration for the provision of food. Independent farmers prospered in times of normal agricultural conditions, but their very independence was an obstacle in times of need. The departure of Elimelech and his family to Moab in search of food may correspond to this reality, and the point of their going to nearby Moab may not be, as is usually assumed, that there was less problem with the production of food there than in Judah, but that the monarchical system of government in Moab coped with the problem better.[52] The experience in Moab would therefore serve to shake confidence in the theocratic form of government Elimelech's family had left behind in Judah, and to introduce them to a monarchical system which, in the matter of the provision of food, proved successful.

The latter success contrasted with the devastation of Elimelech's family line, which Naomi interpreted as God's opposition to it.[53] With the provision of food again in Judah, however, Naomi and Ruth returned home – to the prospect of a future abundance of food and the rebirth of a line that would two generations hence issue in King David. How remarkable that Elimelech's family, whose name stood for loyalty to God as king, which was forced to sojourn in a nation ruled by a human one, is the line that produces the future Israelite king, so that Judah and Israel achieve in time their desire of being ruled like the surrounding nations.[54]

The deity's view of the pressure to appoint a monarch in Israel had been that they were rejecting him as king.[55] Yet, in an apparent contradiction, he ends up agreeing to the request and laying down the rules to govern its institution. Furthermore, he chooses the king and in the choice of David confers sonship upon his lineage.[56] We are justified in explaining such a puzzling development by the notion of a compromise between the ideal order of things and the existing human condition. The deity accommodates himself to human need and weakness.[57] The observation nonetheless stands that his final position of total support and involvement in the establishment of the monarchy means that he has reversed his initial position of antagonism to it.

The story of Ruth may well represent the recognition of the peculiar development of the deity's switch in attitude. It is therefore less bewildering that the deity in the end chooses Elimelech's family line as the one that will give rise to King David. The book will belong to that period of reflection when interpreters faced up to the problem of divine opposition to the kingship, on the one hand, followed by support for its institution, on the other. The contradictory development had to be viewed as somehow divinely directed. The author of Ruth is on the side of earthly kingship but is nonetheless aware of views against it. To reconcile the two positions, he records how the choice of the monarch came from one of those families that had sought to maintain the belief in God as sole king and had therefore originally opposed human kingship. This family's experience in Moab, in a nation ruled by a king, was the catalyst that brought about the change in their destiny. The author's attitude is not far from that which emerges in the Book of Judges: kingship is acclaimed as necessary but the view that it is or can be an evil is not suppressed, as the recording of Jotham's fable makes clear.

ABBREVIATIONS

AB = Anchor Bible
AJT = American Journal of Theology
ATD = Das Alte Testament Deutsch
BJRL = Bulletin of the John Rylands Library
BKAT = Biblischer Kommentar : Altes Testament
CBC = Cambridge Bible Commentary
CH = Code of Hammurabi
ET = English Translation
HL = Hittite Laws
HTR = Harvard Theological Review
ICC = International Critical Commentary
JAOS = Journal of American Oriental Society
JBL = Journal of Biblical Literature
JCS = Journal of Cuneiform Studies
JJS = Journal of Jewish Studies
J. Phil. = Journal of Philology
JQR = Jewish Quarterly Review
JR = Juridical Review
KAT = Kommentar zum Alten Testament
LXX = The Septuagint
MAL = Middle Assyrian Laws
MGWJ = Monatsschrift für Geschichte und Wissenschaft des Judentums
MT = The Massoretic Text
NEB = New English Bible
NTS = New Testament Studies
OED = Oxford English Dictionary
RIDA = Revue internationale des droits de l'Antiquité
RSV = Revised Standard Version
VT = Vetus Testamentum
ZAW = Zeitschrift für die alttestamentliche Wissenschaft

NOTES

INTRODUCTION

1. *The Laws of Deuteronomy* (1974). I have since provided further evidence of this lawgiver's methods of compiling laws: 'A Common Element in Five Supposedly Disparate Laws', *V T* 29 (1979) 129-42.
2. See J. J. Finkelstein, 'Ammiṣaduqa's Edict and the Babylonian "Law Codes"', *JCS* 15 (1961) 103; 'Sex Offenses in Sumerian Laws', *JAOS* 86 (1966) 368; S. Paul, *Studies in the Book of the Covenant in the Light of Cuneiform and Biblical Law* (1970) 23-6. The latter cites the view of F. R. Kraus that the collections use the language typical of hypothetical scribal propositions and therefore constitute an example of Babylonian academic literature.
3. *The Common Background of Greek and Hebrew Civilizations* (1965) 285.
4. Some recent work has sought to understand how the Genesis material has been compiled. See, e.g., J. P. Fokkelman, *Narrative Art in Genesis, Specimens of Stylistic and Structural Analysis* (1975).
5. See in particular M. Weinfeld, *Deuteronomy and the Deuteronomic School* (1972).

CHAPTER ONE
Sarah

1. Gen 12:10-20; 20; 26:1-11.
2. The story in Genesis 20 does not spell out the fact of Sarah's beauty (see later discussion).
3. E. A. Speiser was the first to suggest a link: 'The Wife-Sister Motif in the Patriarchal Narratives', in *Biblical and Other Studies*, ed. A. Altmann (1963) 15-28.

Speiser stresses that the Genesis accounts are at odds with the original historical reality he attempts to construct. The legal practice in question was no longer understood, he argues, when the later biblical writers handled the memory of it – hence the discrepancies.
4. By the time of Deut 27:22, Lev 18:9, 11; 20:17 such a union is considered incestuous and is prohibited. E. R. Leach wrongly assumes that the later levitical law existed in Abraham's time. See 'Genesis as Myth', in *Myth and Cosmos*, ed. J. Middleton (1967) 10.
5. The entry under *Deceptions* is one of the largest in Stith Thompson's *Motif-Index of Folk-Literature*, 6 vols., 1957.
6. This lack of judgment on Abram's action implies sympathy for his plight in foreign parts. The view taken is probably akin to that of the early Romans. Any man sojourning within the bounds of a foreign state was at the mercy of the latter and its citizens. All that belonged to him would be readily appropriated by the first comer, for he was outside the protection of the law. Without some sort of alliance with his group a stranger had no right to claim protection against maltreatment of his person or deprivation of his property. See H. F. Jolowicz, *Historical Introduction to Roman Law* (1952)² 57, 58, 100.
7. Gen 26:11.
8. On the nationalism and anti-Canaanite feeling as the most striking characteristic of Deuteronomy, see R. A. Carlson, *David, the Chosen King* (1964) 26.

9. Deut 24:1-4. The law, however, should not be interpreted as a blanket condemnation of every attempt to renovate a marriage. See later discussion.

10. The law thus opposes the consequence of the deity's intervention in Genesis 12. Pharaoh restored Sarai to Abram after her time (as a wife) with him. The law does not permit such a restoration. We shall see that the law is more aligned to the attitude pervading the account of Sarah's situation with Abimelech in Genesis 20.

11. Joseph torments his brothers by telling them that they have come to Egypt as spies, 'to see the nakedness of the land' (*'erwat ha'areṣ*), Gen 42:9. The reference is to that part of the country which it is not possible to conceal from foreign, inquisitive eyes.

12. A formal factor which accounts for the duplicate use of the expression is that each law heads a series of laws parallel to the other series. See C. M. Carmichael, *The Laws of Deuteronomy* (1974) 207.

13. Good physical appearance is often a matter of some moment, sometimes favourable, e.g. Joseph's, Saul's, David's, Abigail's; other times not, e.g. Absalom's, Adonijah's.

14. Such a concern with her behaviour in public would be very much in line with the shame-cultural bias in a great many of the Deuteronomic laws. See D. Daube, 'The Culture of Deuteronomy', *Orita* (Ibadan) 3 (1969) 27-52.

15. I am not denying that such a case as described in the law could not have arisen in the lawgiver's own time. What I am questioning is, if this contemporary case is the basis of the law, why was it given so much importance as to be set down in the Deuteronomic legislation? What is the problem underlying the rule? The fragmented, isolated concerns of the laws would stand out if we had to look for some contemporary issue, and the many important purposes

that the Deuteronomist sets himself in his composition would be trivialised. If, on the other hand, the law represents a critical perspective on one of the nation's traditions, its significance in terms of deserving a place in the legislation is greatly enhanced.

16. More plausible is R. Yaron's view, 'The Restoration of a Marriage', *JJS* 17 (1966) 1-11: the law is designed to protect the second marriage from interference on the part of the ex-husband who is regretful about having divorced her.

17. Rabbi Meir, in the 2nd century A.D., commissioned one of his disciples to pay court to his wife, Beruriah, not in order that he become her lover, but to test her faithfulness. The result was catastrophic. See D. Daube, *Civil Disobedience in Antiquity* (1972) 32, 33.

Thomas Hardy's novel, *The Mayor of Casterbridge*, centres on the action of a man in dire economic straits letting another have his wife for a sum of money. His subsequent regret and later renovation of the marriage meet with no blessing.

18. The fondling incident in Gen 26:8 is an indication that the patriarch, Isaac in this case, did not wish to lose his wife permanently. He had, of course, only anticipated that he might have to lose her to another man.

19. 'On Divorce in Old Testament Times', *RIDA* 4 (1957) 127-8.

20. R. Yaron's points against understanding the *ratio legis* as designed to deter hasty divorce are entirely appropriate in regard to most divorces. But the oddness of this law is the exceptional circumstances prompting the first divorce. Yaron views the law as dealing initially with an ordinary sequence of events and then as taken up with the exceptional practical problem of protecting the second marriage. His concentration of interest is misplaced but he is correct to seek a peculiar rationale for the law. See 'The Restoration of a Marriage', 4. Yaron (6, 7) takes Philo to task for his philosopher's abstract approach. It is, he thinks, remote from law and reality. Yet Philo (*De Specialibus Legibus*, 3.30-1), in attributing an adulterous motive to the woman (in her first marriage) and a pandering one to the man, is probing in the right direction and concentrating on the part of the law that deserves attention (Num 11:11).

21. Moses claimed that he did not find favour in God's eyes because all the people were complaining about lack of food. The loss of favour was not, at least not directly, personal to him but was linked to his situation.

22. This law, however, is moving in the direction of changing that non-requirement by looking into the reasons for the first divorce.

23. He has to prohibit cultic prostitution, an activity associated with his time (1 Kings 14:24, 15:12, 22:47 (46), 2 Kings 23:7, Hos 4:14.

24. Indeed this feature is very prominent in each episode, Gen 12:16; 20:14; 26:12-14.

25. Deut 22:28, 29.

26. Ex 22:15, 16 (16, 17).

27. See chapter 4.

28. This expression presents an interesting contrast to 'the nakedness of a thing'. Both are concerned with appearances, the former with concealment of something awkward, the latter with its open display. In the former the woman's time with another man not her husband is at issue, in the latter a woman's appeal to another man not her husband.

29. 'The Restoration of a Marriage', 6.

30. Deut 22:22.

31. See chapter 4.

32. Deut 22:12. Cp. the similar law in Num 15:37-9.

33. See D. Daube, 'The Culture of Deuteronomy', 27-52.

34. Deut 25:17-19.

35. e.g. Deut 28:1-14.

36. It is remarkable that both appear to be living in the palace.

CHAPTER TWO
Sarah, Rachel, Leah, and Dinah

1. Apart from their many links with the wisdom tradition, two of them (boundary marks, weights and measures) are similarly expressed in Prov 22:28 (cp. 23:10), 16:11 (cp. 11:1, 20:23).

2. Gen 12:10-20.

3. Gen 26:6-11.

4. Genesis 34.

5. Gen 31:26.

6. Abraham and Isaac feared they would be killed because of their wives, Laban and Jacob were entangled in their mutual provocations, Shechem, Hamor and all their men were dispatched by Simeon and Levi and it emerges that an uneasy relationship already existed between Jacob's group and the other Canaanite groups.

7. Note the emphasis upon seeing the woman in the narratives: 'And when the Egyptians see thee [Sarai]' (Gen 12:12); 'Because she [Rebecca] was fair to look upon' (Gen 26:7); 'And when Shechem saw her [Dinah]' (Gen 34:2).

8. The beauty of Sarai, Rebecca, and Rachel is specifically brought out. The former two are living in foreign territory, the latter will eventually be taken to foreign territory.

9. Recall how for the purposes of his law on the renovation of a marriage the legislator had to ignore the patriarch's lack of legal status abroad.

10. A constant theme in Deuteronomy is that Israel is special, is above all other peoples (e.g. 7:6), and consequently their conduct must be of the highest, above and beyond that of the surrounding nations.

11. It is applied to Joseph in Gen 39:6. Elsewhere it is used of Abigail (1 Sam 25:3) and Esther (Esther 2:7).

12. See chapter 3.

13. See *The Exodus Pattern in the Bible* (1965) 65.

14. And probably not in patriarchal times either, rough and ready customary practice being the rule.

15. On the coming together of life and death which is signified by the rites, and on the reason for the clash with the mourning law in Deut 14:1, see C. M. Carmichael, 'A Common Element in Five Supposedly Disparate Laws', *V T* 29 (1979) 129-42.

16. Abraham's view (stated in Genesis 12, implied in Genesis 20) that when the men see her beauty they will slay him and take her supports this impression.

17. Gen 34:19.

18. To be sure, there is some necessity to insist that the man does not treat her as the equal of a slave. She is without parents and hence no one to watch out for abuse. We have, moreover, to recall the influence of the earlier laws in Ex 21:7-11 which are also opposed to the humiliating treatment of slave concubines. The humiliation in question, however, is not linked, at least not directly, to such concerns.

19. See *Exodus Pattern*, 65, 66. He emphasises, because of a common misunderstanding, that the use of force by the man is not the issue, but the lack of consent from her father or guardian.

20. The term occurs in Deut 21:14 and 22:24, 29, and each time Dinah's situation is in the background. Elsewhere it occurs in Gen 31:50 (Jacob's treatment of Rachel and Leah), Judg 19:24, 2 Sam 13:12, 14, 22, 32, and Ezek 22:10, 11, La 5:11.

21. See C. M. Carmichael, *The Laws of Deuteronomy* (1974) 53-67.

22. *Deuteronomy* ICC (1902) 245-6.

23. The NEB reads $y^e da^c ah$ for $y^{e^c} adah$, i.e., 'has had intercourse with her'.

24. Genesis 37.

CHAPTER THREE
Leah

1. Genesis 48; 49:22-6 and 1 Chron 5:1, 2.

2. Gen 49:2-4; 35:22.

3. Deut 21:15-17.

4. R. Yaron rightly rejects the suggestion of some scholars that $s^e nu^\prime ah$ here means 'divorced'. The term can be technical in reference to divorce but often it is not. To regard it as such in this context would mean that the rule is unnecessarily restrictive: only a first-born son whose mother was divorced could come under it. See 'On Divorce in Old Testament Times', *R I D A* 4 (1957) 119.

5. Further ambivalence about Reuben's inheritance rights might also have been introduced because of the notice in Gen 43:33. At the dinner served in Egypt for Jacob's sons, Reuben is given pride of place at Joseph's table because he is the first-born son.

6. Deut 22:13-19.

CHAPTER FOUR
Dinah, Leah, and Sarah

1. J. Skinner, *Genesis* ICC (1910) 417, 418; G. von Rad, *Genesis* ET (1961) 325. E. A. Speiser, *Genesis* AB (1964) 266-7, attributes the story largely to the J source.

2. Prov 19:11, cp. Prov 16:32 (the one who is slow to anger is preferred to the one who resorts to might); 22:24, 25 (the counsel not to contract friendship with a man given to anger is similar to Jacob's counsel advising against involvement with Simeon and Levi in Gen 49:6).

3. The view that those who engage in violence will be engulfed by it is well expressed in Prov 1:10-19.

4. Gen 49:5-7.

5. Gen 34:30.

6. Deut 33:17, Num 23:22 = 24:8, cp. Num 22:4. Cp. also Num 25:3, Ps 106:28.

7. See the later discussion about Judah's half-Canaanite sons, 62-3.

8. *puṣ*, 'to scatter', is frequently applied to animals and often, as here, the application is figurative, e.g. Jer 10:21, 23:1, 2, Ezek 34:5, Zec 13:7.

9. On the clash between young and old in this narrative in a broader context, see D. Daube, *Civil Disobedience in Antiquity*, 45.

10. Deut 22:10.

11. Traditional Jewish exegesis so interprets it. Unequal strength can also be a problem with two oxen, cp. *Odyssey* 18.372-6.

12. In biblical Hebrew the sense of 'to plough' in Jud 14:18 comes close to the sexual one. For post-biblical Hebrew, see J. Levy, *Wörterbuch über die Talmudim und Midraschim* II (1924)² 117.

13. Note the following examples: 'The first-fruits of his strength' (21:17); 'To uncover his father's skirt' (23:1 [22:30]); 'The wages of a dog' (23:19 [18]); cp. 'Are the trees in the field men that they should be besieged by thee' (20:19).

14. Deut 7:1-3.

15. Gen 34:29, 35:2. I have argued that the two laws about the mixed cloth and the tassels, which precede the law about the non-virginal bride, concern the topic of marriage, especially an Israelite's to the right kind of woman. See *The Laws of Deuteronomy* (1974) 163-6.

16. Jacob's willingness to accept a marriage between Shechem and Dinah is underlined by this fact.

17. Gen 34:7.

18. So A. Phillips, *Deuteronomy* CBC (1973) 148. W. W. Hallo reconstructs an 18th century B.C. case from Nippur which appears to deal with a bride slandered by the bridegroom *before* the consummation of the marriage. In my view he fails to realise how significant the difference is between the Babylonian and the biblical case. His statement that it lies in the mechanics of the judicial process ('Instead of investigating the bridegroom's allegations before consummation of the marriage, the Bible provides for it afterwards.')

is an attempt to minimise the actual difference between the two cases. See, 'The Slandered Bride', in *Studies Presented to A. Leo Oppenheim* (1964) 95-105.

19. By delaying he might hope that the wedding-night sheet no longer existed, but then her loss of virginity would be attributed to him.

20. See R. Yaron, 'On Divorce in Old Testament Times', *RIDA* 4 (1957) 127-8. Z. W. Falk sees his allegation as an attempt to justify divorcing her, *Hebrew Law in Biblical Times* (1964) 155. G. von Rad also gave this reason, *Deuteronomy* ET (1966) 142. Such a view is as old as Philo's, *de Specialibus Legibus* 3.80. Where there is no need to show cause one might expect capricious divorces. Among other factors, however, the loss of the wife's dowry and the expense of a bride-price for a new wife would act as constraints.

21. 'And in the morning, behold, it was Leah' (Gen 29:25).

22. We would have to imagine a situation in which a man felt he had been cheated by a girl's father into marriage with a daughter other than the one he wanted. Presumably there was scope for misunderstanding or cheating because of the lack of a formal, written contract. (Biblical law, unlike other Near Eastern systems, appears not to have used written marriage contracts. See Z. W. Falk, *Hebrew Law*, 152-3.) In Jacob's case we have to reckon with Laban's use of customary law to his own ends (a duty to marry off, he claims, an elder daughter before a younger) and, in addition, the probable fact that Jacob was drunk on the wedding night. Festivities are mentioned and one has to account for his failure to recognise the identity of his bride. From the viewpoint of the biblical narrator (see D. Daube, *Studies in Biblical Law* [1947] 190-200) Jacob was being paid back for cheating his elder brother out of his father's blessing. He had succeeded because of his father's

blindness. Just so, his father-in-law succeeds in cheating him because he is blind drunk. After the event Jacob must have pondered what Laban had been about and one thought may well have been that he was using the opportunity to marry off a daughter who was not a virgin. How far back the custom of exhibiting the wedding-night sheet goes, and therefore of clarifying such matters, is not known. In regard to the law, the man's attack on the girl's virtue would probably be aimed at pressuring the father to take her back. The lawgiver, however, is not adverting to the facts of any case known to him in his time. The one in question is hypothetical and is prompted by reflection on Jacob's relationship to Leah. Any attempt to determine the man's overall intention is too speculative.
23. God compensates Leah, who was after all simply obeying her father, by granting her many children. In Greek mythology the daughters of Danaus who killed their husbands on their wedding night at the behest of their father were punished by having everafter to fill a leaky tub with water. The action symbolises abundant fertility constantly denied. On the figurative use of water in reference to women, see my 'Marriage and the Samaritan Woman', *N T S* 25 (1979) in press.
24. Philo so viewed the man's attack. He also observed that it implied that the father or guardian had cheated and deceived the bridegroom, *de Specialibus Legibus* 3.81.
25. Gen 49:31.
26. As Daube points out, Laban seems to have been fairly certain that Jacob could not send Leah back; otherwise his trick would have been too risky. Moreover, if Jacob had reacted he would have stood to lose Rachel. See *Studies in Biblical Law*, 305n.6.
27. See C. M. Carmichael, *The Laws of Deuteronomy*, 228, 234, 237.

28. Shechem's specific offence consisted in taking Dinah without seeking her father's consent. Simeon and Levi, in turn, did not seek their father's permission in taking action against him.
29. The usual procedure was for the bride to be brought to the husband's house (2 Sam 17:3), presumably before consummation. See Z. W. Falk, *Hebrew Law*, 140.
30. See D. Daube, 'The Self-Understood in Legal History', *Juridical Review* 85 (1973) 129.
31. See C. M. Carmichael, *The Laws of Deuteronomy*, 188-9.
32. Cp. MAL 12 (only the married woman who resists in a populated area); CH 130 (only the betrothed woman who attempted to cry out in her father's house); HL 197 (the married woman who is innocent because ravished in the mountains and the married woman ravished in a house who is accounted guilty).
33. Gen 34:1.
34. This national element already appears in the Genesis narrative. Quite apart from Simeon and Levi's attitude, there is the use of the title Israel in a context in which Jacob is the more natural reference, 'because he [Shechem] had wrought folly in Israel by lying with Jacob's daughter' (Gen 34:7). Israel as a geographical, national entity did not yet exist.
35. This political element in couching a law in cryptic language compares well with the use of fables in antiquity. See D. Daube, *Ancient Hebrew Fables* (1973) 5-32. There is a deliberate ambiguity about a fable's function: its message whilst hidden is often meant to be revealed as well. The setting in which it is used determines where the emphasis lies. For example, if used among slaves, the revelation would be important. If their masters are around, conceal-ment would probably be more important although revelation might be hoped for too. At another social level, an 'in' group, such as

one cultivating special knowledge and wisdom, enjoys communicating in cryptic fashion. At the same time, however, its need to reinforce its sense of superiority requires that the outsider sometimes sees the point as well and, being impressed, will seek admission to the ranks.

CHAPTER FIVE
Bilhah

1. Jacob's name has just been changed to Israel (Gen 35:10).
2. Deut 23:1 (22:30): 'A man shall not take his father's wife, nor shall he uncover his father's skirt.'
3. That is, chapters 12-26. In the list of curses in Deut 27:15-26 this same prohibition is again cited (vs. 20) and is followed by other examples (vss. 22, 23).
4. 'It's no go the Yogi-Man,/it's no go Blatavsky/All we want is a bank balance and a bit of skirt in a taxi' – Louis MacNeice in his poem 'Bagpipe Music'. It continues, 'It's no go the Herring Board,/it's no go the Bible/All we want is a packet of fags when our hands are idle.'
5. In a Bedouin custom a relative of the bridegroom throws a man's coat over the bride and explains how the groom and only he will cover her. See J. L. Burckhardt, *Notes on the Bedouins and Wahábys*, I (1831) 263-4.
6. *The Laws of Deuteronomy* (1974) 163-5.
7. Recall wisdom counsel about enjoying one's wife and avoiding other women, e.g. Prov 5:15-20, Job 31:1, 2, 9-12.
8. The role of opposites in the formulation of a whole range of laws I have worked out in the following: 'A Time for War and a Time for Peace: The Influence of the Distinction upon some Legal and Literary Material', in *Studies in Jewish Legal History in Honour of David Daube*, ed. B. S. Jackson, (1974) 50-63; 'On Separating Life and Death: an Explanation of Some Biblical Laws', *HTR* 69

(1976) 1-7; 'A Common Element in Five Supposedly Disparate Laws', *VT* 29 (1979), 129-42.
9. Deut 33:6.
10. While wisdom counsel is often given to condemning passion it can also be positive, e.g. Prov 5:15-20 (vs. 19, 'And be thou ravished always with her love').

CHAPTER SIX
The Daughters of Lot

1. Gen 19:30-8.
2. Deut 23:3 (2).
3. The lawgiver has occasion to refer to Sodom and Gomorrah (the incident with Lot occurred just after their destruction) in his own material when describing the dire punishments to befall the Israelite nation should they resort to idolatry (Deut 29:22 [23]). The geographical setting for the warning is the land of Moab (28:69 [29:1]).
4. Actually the historical evidence about the treatment of the Israelites at the time of the exodus suggests an opposite point of view. For instance, Deut 2:29 implies (contrary to 23:5 [4]) that the Moabites sold the Israelites bread and water for money. The influence on the Deuteronomist of his negative reaction to the origin of these two groups may explain this discrepancy. See C. M. Carmichael, *The Laws of Deuteronomy* (1974) 175.
5. Eccles 1:15 (what is crooked cannot be made straight), 3:15 (that which is, already has been; that which is to be, already has been).
6. Genesis AB (1964) 143.
7. The question can be left open about whether the compiler of the Genesis material has himself shaped the tradition in this way, or even created it entirely, or whether the tradition existed independently of the Sodom one but began to be linked to it before the compiler's time.
8. Note the English expression, 'blind drunk'. Cp. Prov 23:29-35.

On the link between blindness and drunkenness in regard to Jacob and Judah, see ch.8, n.39.

CHAPTER SEVEN
Tamar

1. E. A. Speiser so views it, *Genesis* AB (1964) 299-300.

2. In Gen 44:16, 17 Judah sought on behalf of his brothers that they all be held responsible for the silver cup that had turned up in Benjamin's sack. Joseph, however, rejected his plea and insisted on Benjamin's guilt alone.

3. This tactic clears them of any liability for Joseph's fate. From the point of view of biblical law his death is to be ascribed to *force majeure* and their presentation of the evidence means that Jacob can do no other but formally acknowledge what it betokens. See D. Daube, *Studies in Biblical Law* (1947) 3-10.

4. His place of residence is Adullam in the Canaanite lowlands, Speiser, *Genesis*, 299.

5. The child born of the union would not be his but his dead brother's. That portion of the estate which would accrue to him because of his brother's death would be lost because of the claims of this heir.

6. Gen 37:27.

7. *'attah* is emphatic. See J. Skinner, *Genesis* ICC (1910) 519.

8. Gen 37:2.

9. Gen 37:4.

10. Gen 37:33.

11. With vowels the spelling is *šēlāh*.

12. The MT has the spelling *šîlōh* but it could also be *šēlāh*. The *plena scriptio* can be disregarded (it is not found in many Mss) and the reading *šlh* has a strong claim to originality. The Targum Yerushalmi and other Jewish sources read *šîlōh* as 'his son, offspring' (probably *šîl* from *šᵉlîl*, but the latter in post-biblical Hebrew only; also influenced by *šilyah* 'afterbirth', Deut 28:57). S. R. Driver thinks that this mean-

ing is embodied in the Massoretic punctuation, see *J.Phil.* 14 (1885) 7. Those ancient authorities who understood it this way are doubtless wrong from a philological point of view, but they are close to the original meaning. Like us they would take the plain sense of Gen 49:10 to be concerned with a descendant who will carry on Judah's family line. It is fairly clear why they avoided taking *šlh* to be Shelah. They would have observed that his role as procreator was pushed aside by Judah. The following line, 'And to him would be the obedience of the peoples', continues the sense of the previous one and refers to the birth of a child to a patriarch. By reading, 'Until his son come', they were making sense of the passage. I assume that they no longer appreciated the ironical, mocking nature of Jacob's words.

13. See E. Good, 'The "Blessing" on Judah, Gen 49:8-12', *JBL* 82 (1963) 429-30. The Targums, the LXX, and the Vulgate all saw in the reference the idea of generation.

14. Hence there is no philological problem in the omission of *'el* plus the woman as object. For this use of *bo'*, note Judah's command to Onan to go into Tamar (Gen 38:8).

15. Sarah's son is to be the ancestor of nations, of future kings of many peoples (Gen 17:16). Jacob himself was the bearer of the promise that peoples and nations would serve and bow down to him (Gen 27:29). As this blessing had come from his aged father before him, so now he at a similar stage in life was about to hand down the blessing to a son chosen by him, and not foisted upon him.

16. The imagery in Ezek 19:10-14 is similar to what is found in the Judah saying: the vine has been destroyed and no strong stem remains, no sceptre for a ruler of Israel. In Ps 80:9-20 (8-19) Israel is described as having been a luxurious vine which, with animals playing a destructive role, was ruined. Ps 128:3 promises that a man's wife will be like a fruitful vine within his house. Job 15:29-35 compare the wicked's barren lot to a vine subject to destructive elements. For more detailed evidence of the wordplays and figurative language in the saying, see C. M. Carmichael, 'Some Sayings in Genesis 49', *JBL* 88 (1969) 438-44.

17. Each produces fruit: the palm-tree, dates, the vine, grapes. Applied to the bride's breasts, the figures of the palm and vine convey the notion of her future fertility.

18. Again we might note an interesting contrast between Judah's fortunes and Joseph's. Tamar's wrongful deed constituted a justifiable one in the end and was the means of the upturn in Judah's fortunes. By contrast, Potiphar's wife's wrongful deed contributed to the (temporary) downfall of Joseph (Gen 39:7).

19. Literary cleverness is an important element in the composition of all of these sayings.

20. See E. Good, 'The "Blessing" on Judah', 432.

21. No wine is mentioned but sheep-shearing was a time of festivity and in two other biblical accounts drunkenness is very much part of the scene (1 Sam 25:2-8, 36, 37, about Nabal, and 2 Sam 13:23-8, about Amnon).

22. The colour white is probably to be associated with fertility (another biblical example is possibly the use of the white spots on the rods that Jacob used in his breeding experiment, Gen 30:37). Black is the colour associated with sterility. For an example from a different culture, see V. W. Turner, *The Ritual Process* (1969) 74.

23. Deut 25:5-10.

24. e.g. T. and D. Thompson, 'Legal Problems in the Book of Ruth', *VT* 18 (1968) 88-90.

25. 'Consortium in Roman and Hebrew Law', *Juridical Review* 62 (1950) 72-4.

26. Deut 21:18-21.

27. And possibly from Tamar too, because she could have reported him to her father-in-law.

28. This is another of the many instances we have found in which divine action in the tradition is translated into human in the law.

29. 'The Culture of Deuteronomy', *Orita* (Ibadan) 3 (1969) 27-52.

30. In English the terms 'skimmington' and 'simpleton' were used originally (the 17th century) to simulate a person's name (e.g. Washington) in order to mock him. In the case of a 'skimmington' the ridicule involved a public ceremony and was directed at a husband or wife where one was unfaithful to, or ill-treated, the other. For examples of such rustic justice, see *The English Dialect Dictionary* (1904) under 'skimmington'.

31. See in particular the evidence cited for shoes and feet in J. Nacht, 'The Symbolism of the Shoe with Special Reference to Jewish Sources', *JQR* 6 (1915-16) 14-22, and L. Levy, 'Die Schuhsymbolik im jüdischen Ritus', *MGWJ* 62 (1918) 182-5.

32. Num 12:14, Isa 50:6, Job 30:10.

33. He is a Tannaite of the early part of the 2nd century A.D. I am indebted to Dr Isaac Gottlieb of the University of Beersheba, Israel, for drawing my attention to the passage. Only the edition of H. S. Horovitz and L. Finkelstein (1939, repr. 1969) par. 291, p. 310, includes it (*r' yišma'el 'omer ḥᵃliṣah bišᵉkibah urᵉqiqah kᵉde šikbat zeraʿ*). In M. Friedmann's edition (1864) par. 291, p. 126a, we have instead *r' yišma'el 'omer ḥᵃliṣah mᵉ'akebet urᵉqiqah mᵉ'akebet* (Rabbi Ishmael says, 'Removal is indispensable and spitting is indispensable'.) Another example of the transferred sense of spittle is in *b Niddah* 16b, 'While the spittle is yet in the vagina'.

34. Ex 4:25, Deut 28:57 (female), 2 Kings 18:27 = Isa 36:12, Isa 7:20, Ezek 16:25 (female). Jer 2:25 has, 'Keep thy feet from going unshod and thy throat from thirst', which is an appeal to Israel to cease behaving like a lusty female animal giving herself to any partner. She should have remained bound to her first love, God.

35. Gen 49:10.

36. 2 Sam 11:8, 11.

37. Ex 4:25.

38. Ruth 4:7-10.

39. Song of Songs 4:12.

40. Gen 35:11 (in a blessing of future fertility for Jacob, 'a nation and a company of nations shall be of thee, and kings shall come out of thy loins'), 1 Kings 8:19=2 Chr 6:9.

41. Deut 25:11, 12.

42. It owes something also to the earlier law in Ex 21:22-5, a miscarriage caused by two men fighting. The Deuteronomist is continually alert to contrasting situations. For the link between the two laws, see C. M. Carmichael, *The Laws of Deuteronomy* (1974) 232-5.

43. The law is *not* concerned with damage to a man's testicles. Cp. MAL 8 which details penalties for this kind of injury inflicted by a woman.

44. This transferred meaning (from the agricultural process of producing seed) is found in most cultures. The OED lists the obsolete 'to tread', transitively with 'out', as 'to engender, beget [offspring]'. For 'dreschen', see J. and W. Grimm, *Deutsches Wörterbuch*, 11 (1860) 1403.9. For post-biblical *duš*, J. Levy, *Wörterbuch über die Talmudim und Midraschim*, 1, 388. It is said of Onan in *Genesis Rabbah* 85, 'He trod within but ejaculated without'. See C. M. Carmichael, '"Treading" in the Book of Ruth', *ZAW* 92 (1980).

45. I. M. Casanowicz claims that there are some 27 cases of paronomasia in Deuteronomy, e.g., *sorer umoreh* and *zolel weʾsobeʾ* in 21:18, 20, 'Paronomasia in the Old Testament', *JBL* 12 (1893) 166. The use of *ḥašal* in Deut 25:18, about how the Amalekites shattered the Israelites, may have been prompted by the use of *ḥalaš* in Ex 17:13, about Joshua's disabling the Amalekites. In Deut 8:3, *kol moṣaʾ* 'all that proceeds', is possibly a play upon *kol hamiṣwah* in Deut 8:1, 'every commandment'.

46. It is, however, true that Judah's line was continued by a child born of a Canaanite mother. There is some indication, as we shall see in the next chapter, that Tamar's background was played down and, in a way, also overcome. The ambiguity that continued to attach itself to Judah's situation would also have prompted the law on the unmuzzling of an ox (as against the implied muzzling of an ass).

47. His law about the sale of a brother Israelite in Deut 24:7 stems from his critical scrutiny of the sale of Joseph in Gen 37:26-8.

CHAPTER EIGHT
Ruth

1. Goethe regarded the entire book, 'als das lieblichste kleine Ganze, das uns episch und idyllisch überliefert worden ist'.

2. 'Now when I passed by thee, and looked upon thee, behold, thy time was the time of love; and I spread my skirt over thee, and covered thy nakedness: yea, I sware unto thee and entered into a covenant with thee, saith the Lord God, and thou becamest mine.'

3. Deut 23:1 (22:30): 'A man shall not take his father's wife, nor uncover his father's skirt.'

4. See n.44, chapter 7.

5. Cp. the English idiom cited in the OED, 'To tread one's shoe awry', which signifies 'to fall from chastity.'

6. Ruth 4:15, 17.

7. Already observed by D. F. Rauber, 'Literary Values in Ruth', *JBL* 89 (1970) 35.

8. The legal symbolism has to be explained but not the sexual symbolism involving treading and the sandal, because it was understood.

9. He *goes into* her, 'feetwise' (Ruth

4:13).

10. In Ruth 1:5 there is the curious use of *yeled* and not *ben* in the statement that Naomi was bereft of her two sons and her husband. The use of the former brings out the author's basic concern with fertility, with that which comes out of the womb.

11. From *parah* 'to bear fruit' which is often used to indicate human fertility: e.g., in Gen 26:22, Ex 23:30, Jer 3:16, Ezek 36:11. The blessing upon Boaz in Ruth 4:11, 'And make strength in Ephrathah' refers to his future progeny. For *ḥayil* here as 'procreative power' see C. J. Labuschagne, 'The Crux in Ruth 4:11', *ZAW* 79 (1967) 364-7. The designation 'Ephrathites' causes commentators difficulties.

12. The artificial character of the story is marked, a feature brought out in different ways by, e.g., G. Gerlemann, *Ruth* BKAT, 18/1 (1965) 14; S. Bertman, 'Symmetrical Design in the Book of Ruth', *JBL* 84 (1965) 165-8. The manifold symbolism also points in this direction. The names in the book are commonly regarded as artificial constructions. Even where it is thought that the names might be historical their meanings are still taken to be significant.

13. E. Robertson was puzzled by this contrast: 'The Plot of the Book of Ruth', *BJRL* 32 (1949-50) 209

14. 'Symmetrical Design', 165-8.

15. See J. G. Frazer, *The Golden Bough* (in 1 volume, 1928), chapters on the corn-mother and corn-maiden, in particular, 410-12.

16. It might well be pondered why she there and then beat out the measure of grain. She could have waited till a later time. Expediency does not necessarily explain her action.

17. Ruth 1:6-8.

18. Ruth 1:6-12.

19. Commentators have been struck by the frequency of the repetition of *šub*: E. F. Campbell,

Ruth AB (1975) 79; H. W. Hertzberg, *Die Bücher Josua, Richter, Ruth* ATD, 9 (1959)² 265.

20. Song of Songs 7:2-10 (1-9).

21. Already noted by W. Rudolph, *Das Buch Ruth, Das Hohe Lied, Die Klagelieder* KAT, 17/1-3 (1962) 171-2.

22. *b Niddah* 41b. See J. Levy, *Wörterbuch über die Talmudim und Midraschim*, 1 (1963) 403.

23. Evidence for the legal effect of treading is found in the Nuzi tablets, see E. R. Lacheman, 'Note on Ruth 4:7-8', *JBL* 56 (1937) 53-6; also in Roman Law, *Digest* 41.2.3.1.

24. Ruth 3:10.

25. Gen 38:26.

26. The nearer kinsman willingly responded to the request to redeem Elimelech's land. In that the levirate institution was a dead letter in situations where there was no recognised head of a family to compel compliance, the kinsman need not anticipate any request to perpetuate Elimelech's family line. He could reckon on obtaining the land without further obligation.

27. Its other use in 1 Sam 21:3(2) and 2 Kings 6:8 is about a secret place. The probably contracted form of the expression in Dan 8:13, 'Then I heard a holy one speaking; and another holy one said to the *certain one* who spoke', is only marginally comparable to the expression in Ruth.

28. *Ruth*, 13, 14.

29. It is just possible that the names Mahlon and Chilion, which by etymology suggest sickness and feebleness respectively, are intended, through assonance, to convey the specific suggestion of the disappearance of *'ôn*, 'virility'. On the use of word-play in another area, compare the Shakespearian example in *The Merchant of Venice*, Act 3, Scene 2. To win Portia her suitors had to choose the correct casket out of three, gold, silver, and lead. Two of the suitors were unsuccessful, gold and silver constituting the wrong choice.

Bassanio is the next suitor and we already know that he and Portia had met previously and had responded to each other. But like the others he had to choose correctly. While he is deliberating Portia has some music played: 'Tell me where is fancy *bred*,/Or in the heart or in the *head*?/How begot, how nourish*ed*?/Reply, reply./'It is engender'd in the eyes,/With gazing *fed*; and fancy dies/In the cradle where it lies./ Let us all ring fancy's knell:/I'll begin it, – Ding, dong, bell.' He chooses lead. To return to the word-play involving Onan. One possibility is '*ōnî*, '*ōnî*, 'my virile one, my virile one'. Another is '*ōn-* '*ōn* to rhyme with '*ōnān* or, a distinct possibility because of the Massoretic use of *qāmeṣ* for both the long *ā* sound and the short *o* sound, with '*ōnon*.

30. The *hiphil* of *šḥt* refers to the destruction of nature in Deut 20:19, 20, Jud 6:4, Mal 3:11. Jeremiah is compared to a fruit-bearing tree which his enemies wish to destroy so that his name will disappear (Jer 11:19).

31. *An Introduction to the Books of the Old Testament* (1958) 84.

32. Professor Daube kindly forwarded to me his chapter on Ruth from his forthcoming book on *Ancient Jewish Law*.

33. The book of Ruth is set in the period of the Judges. Recent work has produced convincing arguments why the book should not be dated in later, post-exilic times (a view widely accepted in critical scholarship), but in pre-exilic, even Solomonic times. See R. M. Hals, *The Theology of the Book of Ruth* (1969) 65-75; Campbell, *Ruth*, 23-8; D. A. Leggett, *The Levirate and Goel Institutions in the Old Testament* (1974) 143-63.

34. F. Buhl pointed out that he would have the use of the field for many years before the son by the levirate union was old enough to take it for himself. The view that his eventual loss would strain his

own resources is therefore weak. See, 'Some Observations on the Social Institutions of the Israelites', *AJT* I (1897) 736.

35. Gen 38:9. In 2 Sam 14:4-11 the threatened death of the widow's son at the hands of her relatives will mean the destruction of an inheritance and the death of her husband's name (vs. 7).

36. If, with the LXX, we accept '*oz* as part of the name then its use in such texts as Ezek 19:11, 12, 14, in reference to Israel's failure to become a strong royal line, is especially revealing because the notion of procreative strength is uppermost. M. Noth, *Die israelitischen Personennamen im Rahmen der gemeinsemitischen Namengebung* (1928) 228, gives a different basis for the name. He nonetheless comes up with the meaning 'vigorous'.

37. I Kings 14:24, 15:12, 22:47 (46), 2 Kings 23:7, Hos 4:14. See S. R. Driver, *Deuteronomy* ICC (1902) 264-5, and M. Astour, 'Tamar the Hierodule', *JBL*, 85 (1966) 185-96.

38. Ruth 1:16, 17.

39. Wine seems to play a role in each seduction. Jacob's description of Judah's eyes ('*enayim*) being red with wine (Gen 49:12) is a reference to Judah's time with the prostitute at Enaim ('*enayim*, Gen 38:14). Sheep-shearing is a time of feasting according to I Sam 25:2-8, 36, 37 and 2 Sam 13:23-28. Nabal and Amnon's drinking on these two occasions had disastrous consequences for them. Jacob himself in failing to recognise Leah on his wedding night may have been drunk. A banquet had just been concluded.

40. So M. Astour, 'Tamar the Hierodule', 185-96. The sacred prostitute could marry but she must not bear children. If married she wore a veil, unlike the common prostitute. Astour's evidence is from Assyro-Babylonian sources.

41. Judah attended to the harlot's payment the next day, just as on the day after their sexual encounter Boaz completed his arrangement with Ruth.

42. So E. Good, 'The "Blessing" on Judah, Gen 49:8-12', *JBL* 82 (1963) 429. J. Emerton rejects the further links (not necessary for the point in question) Good seeks to make with the references to the other terms for staff in Gen 49:10, see 'Some Difficult Words in Genesis 49', in *Words and Meanings*, eds. P. R. Ackroyd and B. Lindars (1968) 85.

43. Tamar was the means by which Judah's vine was to produce new branches. She was not the vine itself.

44. The treading upon the grapes is vividly conveyed in Gen 49:11. From the viewpoint of viticulture the treading comes at the wrong stage, before the grapes have been harvested and put in the winepress. Moreover, asses would not be used for the proper work of treading. At the figurative sexual level, the description of what takes place is singularly appropriate. It is well-recognised that terms for intercourse often have a violent meaning. For example, in biblical material, 'to plough' and 'to tread' are employed this way (Ps 129:3, Amos 1:3).

45. See n.33.

46. Deut 23:4-7 (3-6).

47. For a similar process in another biblical narrative, see D. Daube, *Studies in Biblical Law* (1947) 157.

48. As noted in a previous chapter, Deuteronomy is fashioned as a farewell speech by Moses who, like Jacob in Genesis 49, surveys the past events of the life and experience of the children of Israel with a view to determining their future well-being. He is especially interested in the events that occurred during his own life, for example, the behaviour of the Ammonites and Moabites at the time of the exodus from Egypt (Deut 2:8-37, 23:4-7 [3-6]).

49. Or simply 'God is King'. The *i*-vowel may not represent a pronominal suffix: see M. Noth, *Die Personennamen*, 34, 35. The name occurs nowhere else in biblical material. On the one hand, the term *'el* would mean the Israelite god, on the other, it could be viewed as less than satisfactory because of its association with foreign gods.

50. I am concerned with the final shape of the book of Ruth but I incline to the view of W. Rudolph, *Das Buch Ruth*, 70 (and others, Hals, *Theology*, 15, Gerlemann, *Ruth*, 7) that the reference to David in 4:17 is authentic. Even if it were not one would still wish to know what was intended by its addition.

51. Jud 7:9-21. Like so much of the symbolic language in the book of Ruth, the language of the fable is borrowed from the agricultural world.

52. This view would resolve the problem which G. Gerlemann (*Ruth*, 14) raises, namely, that it is quite unrealistic to expect no famine in Moab at a time when there is one in the same geographical region of Judah. We might also recall Joseph's successful attempt to centralise the distribution of grain in Egypt (Gen 41:25-57).

53. Ruth 1:21.

54. It is noteworthy that David's own parents stayed with the king of Moab (1 Sam 22:3).

55. 1 Sam 8:4-22.

56. 1 Sam 9:15-10:25 (Saul), 2 Sam 7:14 (sonship and David's line).

57. On the prevalence of this idea in biblical material, see D. Daube, 'Concessions to Sinfulness in Jewish Law', *JJS* 10 (1959) 1-3; C. M. Carmichael, 'A Common Element in Five Supposedly Disparate Laws', *VT* 29 (1979) 129-42.

INDEX OF SOURCES

SUBJECT INDEX